NOT TOO BAD

From the Diaries of a 1970s Teenage Brummie

by
Paul Duffin

Cover design by Claire Duffin

©2016 Paul Duffin

PREFACE

I decided to write this book for several reasons. First of all, I still had my complete diaries for the five years from 1970 to 1974. I was always a bit of a "stato" i.e. interested in statistics, usually sport related, but my diaries revealed far more, such as pints drank and pubs visited, bands seen etc. I had made a few entries in a diary for the year before (1969) but the full daily reports only started in January 1970 when I was sixteen and in the middle of my 'O' level year. They finished at the end of 1974 when I made a major career change.

The second reason was due to my health. I retired in 2002 as a result of losing the sight in my good eye (the left). The inflammation that caused the problem has now spread to affect both my optic and auditory nerves leading to very poor vision and hearing. This has restricted what I can do but with the aid of a computer I can write.

My intention is to both entertain and shed some light on growing up in Birmingham in the early 1970's. I also intend it to be an accurate account and as such anything you see in *italics* is a direct quote from a diary. I hope that no one is embarrassed or offended as this is certainly not my intention.

I am writing primarily for myself plus of course friends and family. It will be a bonus if anyone else enjoys it. All money raised (after costs) will go to Guide Dogs, who do such fantastic work with the visually impaired.

I have received lots of help from friends and family. A big "thank you" to my editorial assistants; Liz Lavender and Andy Bates. They have been both diligent and highly effective. I have also received help from my old friends John Lavender and Gary Durant who both kept diaries for some of the years. Also thanks to everyone who has put up with my constant references to "the book", particularly my wife Sue.

Paul Duffin: September 2016

INTRODUCTION

I grew up at 9 Charminster Avenue, Yardley, a blue-collar suburb of Birmingham in a conventional three bed semi built in 1939 by Dares the well-known local builder. We moved there in 1954 when I was just a year old from Freer Road Handsworth near the Aston Villa football ground, to be in a "better area".

All went well as I glided through life with an almost constant smile until February 1969. At just forty eight, on his way to work, my Dad (Stan) collapsed and died of a heart attack. My brother Steve was with him, having recently started work at Lloyds Bank in the centre of Birmingham. It was a terrible shock for everyone as this was his first and last heart attack. It would take a while for my smile to return, but it did.

I was at school that day and came home as usual at about 4.30 pm. My football team Aston Villa had recently progressed to the fifth round of the FA Cup and were due to play away from home at Spurs at the weekend. I had bought a ticket and booked a coach seat with friends. I came into the house singing Villa songs, full of joy. I was surprised to see my Nan and Grandpa, plus my Mum's sister, Aunt Joyce sitting in the dining room drinking tea. "Family gathering!" I declared, but Mum and Aunt Joyce revealed the awful truth calmly and lovingly. "Where's Steve?"I blurted out. It transpired he had been given tranquillisers and kept at the hospital for a few hours to recover from the shock

My Nan never really got over losing her only son. She died within a couple of years, a broken woman. We were a small family and matters were made much worse by my Aunt Joyce and Uncle Cyril's pending retirement to the Isle of Man. They didn't leave until later that year but were committed to the move by the time Dad died. Mum had a hysterectomy in the May. All in all it was a terrible time.

Our house was situated on what we referred to as the "square". Just past the Yew Tree was Stoney Lane, part of the outer circle bus route (number 11). The first left turn was Rockingham Road, which formed one side of the square. Heathmere Avenue formed two sides with my side, Charminster completing the set up.

This was home to lots of kids of my age. On Rockingham were John Lavender (John L) and Brian Harris (Bri). At the top of Heathmere were Steve Clayton (Steve C) and Alan Horton. At the end of Heathmere was Andrew Bullock who had the added benefit of access to the cricket field at the bottom of his garden. Back on Stoney Lane, backing on to my house were Paul Wells (Shrimp), Gary Durant (Gaz) and Terry Twinberrow (Tez).

Our next door neighbours were the Beresfords: Mum and Dad- Eric and Marjorie plus children Joy and Richard. A lovely family and great neighbours. Marjorie's sister Eileen, husband Gordon and children Ann, Jane and Tim (the Yardley's) lived a few roads away. For as long as I can remember I always wanted to be part of a large family. The Beresfords and the Yardleys belonged to an evangelical church near The Swan, and Steve and I were taken to "Sunday school" by the Beresford's from a very young age. In many ways, both of these lovely families became my larger family for many years to come.

CHAPTER ONE 1970: A year of firsts

Lots of things happened in the world at large in 1970: The Vietnam war, now fifteen years old, continued at a tireless pace; and a cyclone in Bangladesh killed over half a million people. A year after the first moon landing Apollo 13 grabbed the world's attention as it made its way back to earth after a troubled flight. Intel invented the memory chip, lead free petrol was developed and bar codes came into being. The world of entertainment saw the Beatles split; Jimi Hendrix, aged just 27, passed on in a Purple Haze; and disco dancing 'hustled' its way on to the world stage. In sport Brazil won the World Cup and Joe Frazier became heavyweight boxing champ.

Back in the UK the age of majority was lowered from 21 to 18; opinion polls wrongly predicted a Labour victory in the general election as Heath beat Wilson; and BP struck oil in the North Sea although it took them another 5 years to start pumping the oil back to the mainland.

Even closer to home in Yardley, my world was dominated by a year of firsts: a pint in a pub; a 'proper' girlfriend; a party with neither parents nor jelly; a rock band gig; plus a whole lot more.

1970 KICKS OFF

For several years my brother Steve and I were invited to the Yardley's New Year's Eve parties. December 31st 1969 was no exception as family and friends gathered to welcome in the new decade and my 1970 diary was launched;

Thursday 01.01.70…. *"Arrived home 1.25 am"*.

Not exactly Samuel Pepys but a start.

1970 was my 'O' level year at Central Grammar School for Boys Tile Cross and with the start of the new term in January along came our "mocks". I should have been well into revision at this stage, but such was my perpetual state of optimism that I hadn't quite started;

Friday 09.01.70.... *"revised Geog, but not for very long"*

The 'O' level pass rate at the time was said to be about 45%. My best result was 46% in geography (all that revision paid dividends!), my worst was French at 14% (oh la la!). This should have been a severe warning and a call for action. However, my response on receiving the damning report was a little different;

Friday 13.02.70.... *"had reports NOT TOO BAD. Had my hair cut".*

Optimism 1: Attitude to study 0. Does my attitude to study change? We'll see.

PARTIES WITHOUT JELLY

I am now sixteen years old my hair is daringly just over my collar even after returning from Kent's, the barbers at the Yew Tree. My first real party (where jelly is replaced by beer and parents are absent) takes place at the home of my best school friend Mark Ford.

Not unlike many school friendships it began with an altercation in a German lesson when we were about thirteen. Mark was taller and stronger than me, but somewhat out of character I punched him on the nose. This impulsive action drew the difference of opinion to a close, and gained his undeserved but continued respect.

Mark and his elder brother Paul lived in a maisonette above a row of shops on Tile Cross Road. There were two separate flights of stairs, one at each end of the shops. On the night of the party we had strict instructions to wait at one of the staircases for the 'all clear', which meant that Mark's mum and dad had left the building. The call came and the brothers Ford ushered us in.

There were to be more such parties at the Ford residence. They were *always* fun and the brothers provided the undeniable bonus of not only knowing, but also being able to attract GIRLS. My diary entry is brief but interesting. NB: the party was on a Sunday, mid term;

Sunday 25.01.70…. *"Mark's party. Good. 4 pints – Yvonne. Got home about 11.30."*

Did I mention, Mark's parties were always 'good', and at the tender age of sixteen, four pints (at best an optimistic estimate) sounds a little on the high side However, Yvonne (Curtis) I remember well. Lovely girl with dark hair and pretty features. All good so far but at that time despite being only about fourteen or so I seem to remember she smoked which was a real turn off. It turned out she went to Saltley Grammar and was there with her best friend Elaine (Jenkins). We will hear much more of the Saltley girls.

That week turned out to be busy with new adventures. Suspecting that I had done OK in my mocks, I was having some well-deserved fun starting with my first visit to Burney Lane Youth Club. Situated close to Saltley Grammar School it attracted attendees from both Central (all boys) and Saltley (mixed) schools. Two days after Mark's party I am there, and so is Yvonne;

Tuesday 27.01.1970…."*went to the club at Burney Lane. Played table tennis. Deafed Yvonne".*

What a horrible expression -"deafed" (dumped) - but it was of its time. The youth club was run by the church (Christ Church) and focused on table tennis and snooker on a very small table. It bravely also ran discos on occasional Saturdays. The very next evening (Wednesday) saw another new event: a disco for under 18s at the BRS (British Road Services) on Bromford Lane, Hodge Hill;

Wednesday 28.01.1970 ....*'Went to the BRS. It was free to get in. It was good. Danced"*.

With all this socialising diary entries necessarily remained brief with no mention of who else was there. This does change eventually but not yet. As we move to the end of a very busy week, Saturday brings another house party on Sheldon Heath Road, this time hosted by Elaine, friend of Yvonne and one of the 'Saltley girls';

Saturday 31.01.1970...."*Party at Elaine's. She has a colour television. Watched the rugby".*

Doesn't say much for the party if I watched the rugby. But a colour television in January 1970 was a rarity. This girl was 'interesting' and not just because of the colour TV. Returning to the BRS the following week we were shocked that we had to pay an entrance fee after the first week being free, but it was worth it;

Wednesday 04.02.1970 ...."*Went to BRS 2/6 in. It was good. Elaine"*

Thus started a relationship between two youngsters that continued for quite a while.

Number one in the charts from the week before, right up until 3rd of March was Love Grows Where My Rosemary Goes by Edison Lighthouse. Whenever I hear that song my mind drifts back to happy times at the BRS and my FPGF (first proper girlfriend). Everyone had their own definition of what constitutes a 'proper' girlfriend, but mine was simply one where you actually went on "dates", even paying for the other person on occasion, and being more than just friends!

We only went to the BRS on two more occasions. The first on Elaine's birthday (25th Feb); and the last time on 1st April, the day Elaine came back from a school trip to Germany. Gifts were given on her birthday;

Wednesday 25.02.1970...."*Elaine's birthday. Start of the strike. Went to BRS with Tez, Brian, Gaz and Elaine. Scarf, watch strap, chocs".*

The strike referred to is the teachers' strike which was on and off during the whole year. The dispute was about pay and saw the start of a more appropriate remuneration for teachers. More importantly we now have mention of others; Tez is Terence Twinberrow a 6ft 6-inch gentle giant who lived a couple of doors from Gaz (Gary Durant) on Stoney Lane, at the back of my house. Brian (Harris) lived across the road from me on Rockingham Road. John (Lavender) whom we will hear more later lived next door to Brian. We were all good friends and remain so to this day.

Looking at the list of birthday gifts it is easy to fall into the trap of assuming that they were presents from me to Elaine. I am not so sure. OK the chocolates are a pretty safe bet, but a watch strap? You have known a girl for a couple of weeks and you buy her a watch strap? I don't think so. I have a vague recollection that the watch and the scarf (my Dad's) were mine and they were exchanged temporarily as some expression of affection! We were only kids and cash was limited. However, I was soon to be a 'working' man.

IT'S ALL AT THE CO-OP

Apart from a brief spell at the India Tyre and Rubber Company after leaving Aston Commercial school my dad, Harold Stanley Duffin (known as Stan), worked all his life in administration for the Birmingham Co-op. Dad's work colleague and best friend was Peter Muddiman. They also played cricket together and Peter and his wife Hilda lived with my Mum and Dad for a while in Freer Road after they got married. They were close family friends and were known to my brother and I as Uncle Peter and Auntie Hilda. Uncle Peter was the reason my brother and I went to Central Grammar School as he and his twin brother (who unfortunately was killed in the 2nd WW) both went there. Uncle Peter kept an eye on us after Dad died and when I was looking for some income he was only too pleased to find me a Saturday job at the Co-op.

I had experienced working at the Co-op a couple of years before when Dad found me a few hours on a Saturday morning helping out in the shoe department at the High Street store while he worked in the offices above. The law limited the number of hours you could work at fourteen to three or four per day. It was certainly an experience working with older men and the mickey taking was constant but mostly good humoured and a good grounding. For example, one of the lads suggested I would learn everything I needed to know about the facts of life by reading the insert in his packet of condoms. If you have ever bothered to read the small print supplied, you would learn nothing other than they themselves were a pretty good contraceptive by quickly sending you to sleep.

I was taught how to sell and given an early introduction to sales targeting. In the stock room certain shoe boxes had stickers on the outside. If you sold a pair from such a box a small bonus would be paid provided you removed the sticker and presented it to the manager. It was quite amusing trying to convince customers that they should be interested in footwear that had long been out of fashion, if indeed ever in. The best part of the day was break time. The staff canteen was well stocked and I loved the cheese and onion cobs. I can taste them now.

Uncle Peter found me a Saturday job (all day) at the Co-op supermarket at Pool Way shopping precinct on the Medway, Kitts Green. At the time there was a gang from that area known as the Pool Way Mob. I had assumed that this was a mob lead by PAUL WAY until I worked there. Stupid boy!

It was a large store with most staff working full time, although there was one other Saturday boy, I think called Geoff, who introduced me to Led Zeppelin and lent me Led Zepp 2. It wouldn't be too long before I got a bit closer to Led Zepp. The manager was Mr Fox who never left his glass sided office overlooking the checkouts; and hardly ever spoke to anyone apart from his trusty "charge hand" Mr Rooke (unaffectionately known as Rooky by the rest of us). I am not sure why but Rooky and I never really hit it off. Maybe he saw me as some sort of "spy" planted by Head Office due to my connection with Uncle Peter. He did however agree to me leaving early on a Saturday when Villa were at home as long as I worked the missing hours on the night before. He wasn't all bad.

One day Rooky set me the task of restocking one of the chiller cabinets with margarine. All the packs came in twin cartons which then had to be opened to stock the single packs. The cardboard packaging was then discarded. I noticed there was an offer on the twin packs for Zorbit towels. I simply had to save the tokens printed on the packs and send them off and back would come a brand new quality towel. It was all totally legitimate and I soon became the guardian of the chillers. I was restocking like mad and I think Rooky found it hard to see why I was so keen. At home the postman also noticed a change with deliveries to our house, there were also more deliveries to all our friends and relatives. In a few short weeks, it was raining towels.

With 'O' Levels and the cricket season approaching I thought it best to hand in my notice, working at the store for the last time on 11th April. I am not sure which I saw as more important, the cricket or the exams, but I did not work again until after the exams finished at the end of June. By July cricket and exams were over and Uncle Peter came up trumps again this time securing me a position at the Co-op in town. Not retail this time but helping out in the Oak Restaurant situated in the basement of the department store a couple of levels below the footwear department. The manager was Dennis Downing a well spoken affable chap who had known my Dad for many years. The head chef, Lloyd was friendly and well organised. Much nicer than your Gordon Ramsey types but this was the Co-op not The Ivy. The only stars we saw were the hanging ones at Xmas.

The kitchen supervisor was Cis. Now she could have given Gordon Ramsey a run for his money in the temper tantrum stakes, but it was not an easy role as hundreds of meals were served on busy days. Her bark was worse than her bite and we got on OK. I spent many hours on the automated washing machine. It was a cross between a train set and a miniature car wash. About half a dozen trays of plates etc moved slowly along a track through a tunnel, which sprayed, then blow dried each compartment. If you were lucky it would be operated by two people, with one at each end. Often I would be both a putter on'er and a taker off'er. It could be exhausting with temperatures often reaching over a hundred. After a few consecutive days on the machine I would wake up in the middle of the night thinking I was still operating the machine. Very strange.

Jim was in charge of the internal chip "shop". It was just like a chip shop except there were no customers waiting just shouts from below for "more chips" or "more fish". Jim was not young and spoke very little. However, he taught me how to dip the fish in batter and then smoothly glide them on to the surface of the hot fat. It was a skill that took me minutes to perfect. What didn't go quite so well was peeling the potatoes ready for chipping. We had a peeling machine. Basically, it was a round drum with a lid. Jim's instructions were to take the large bag of potatoes and pour them into the top having removed the lid. Begin the water flow, replace the lid and switch on.
Everything done I sat back to wait for them to peel. And they did. Unfortunately, I was distracted and by the time I looked they had all been so well peeled there was nothing, and I mean nothing left. Lesson learnt.

CLUBBING IT

By February Burney Lane (BL) youth club had become a regular slot on a Tuesday night. I was usually joined by Gaz, Tez, Bri, Mark and of course Elaine. The 'Saltley' girls would be there with Yvonne and Elaine now joined by Fiona (Weller), Ann (Jackson), another Elaine (Smith) plus occasionally Margaret and Sue (Clarke). A number of Central lads from my year would also be there. Keith Florey (Floss), Rob Turley, Clive Turvey (aka Scruff, because he always dressed smartly), Dave Barley, and Paul Walker. The usual games of table tennis were accompanied by games of snooker on the very small table. On a couple of Saturdays, the club put on a disco which frankly brought out the worst in some people and attracted the attention of more disruptive elements. The first BL disco was on Saturday 21st February. My only diary reference concerned one of the lads from our year at Central;

Saturday 21.02. 1970.... *"went to Burney Lane disco (joke) with Elaine. (Walker broken).*

I remember Paul Walker being visibly upset. I was told he liked Elaine, which I was unaware of. My other strong memory of the BL discos was the unique dancing style of Chris Hurst. He was at his best dancing to current reggae hits such as 'Long Shot Kick de Bucket' and the 'Liquidator'. With his fists clenched and held as if he was milking a cow. He would then shuffle along. A John Sargent in the making.

I would make the trip to Burney Lane some seventeen times between January and August. Then "clubs" became pubs. But before this progression we also used to go to a couple of other similar "clubs", Long Meadow school disco and Rowlands Road youth club disco. The 'Saltley' girls must have introduced long Meadow girl's school to us. I went with Elaine each of the half dozen times and the only remarkable thing was that I walked her home on at least two occasions. Why remarkable? Well it was a long way from Long Meadow to my house via Sheldon Heath Road but I obviously cared.

Rowlands Road was much nearer to home, just a few minutes' walk, kicking off in June with a really good first night with great music. I can recall lots of us sitting on the floor "freaking out" (well doing something) to "Spirit in the Sky' by Norman Greenbaum which had been at number one the previous month. There was an amazing turn out; The 'Saltley' girls, Elaine, Yvonne, Sue, Margaret, plus the local lads, Gaz, Tez, Bri, John L, Paul Wells (affectionately known as Shrimp) Mark and Paul Ford,), Lil Whitehouse, Jock Brooks, Andrew Farley, Steve Martin, Scruff, Bob T, Pritchard, to name but a few.

BUT the same night Elaine and I had our first argument. It was so momentous that it warranted a separate write up in my diary:

Friday 26.06. 1970.... "*Had a disagreement with Elaine. She complained I didn't pay enough attention to her tonight. She also objected to the continual presence of Gaz, Brian and Tez. She annoyed me with some unnaturally (for her) snide comments. Still, we settled it and she apologised and said it was just a mood. She was also fed up with everything apart from me. She also said that Brian looked 17 (small joke). Went in the Yew Tree before the dance and had half a bitter and lime*"

Well that told me. She was certainly right about the "continual presence" and I was probably paying too much attention to my moves at the disco. We were very young!

It would be six months before we returned to Rowlands Road only to find that the venue had been taken over by "*skinheads and bop music*". Disgusted we moved straight on to the Good Companions pub on the Coventry Road. The Disco must have been really bad as the "Goodies" was a proper drinking pub (i.e. very 'basic', otherwise known as a real dump). We never went back and the pub became a Harry Ramsdens before eventually being replaced by a Travelodge.

MORE PARTIES WITHOUT JELLY

When we weren't "clubbing" we seemed to be meeting up in large groups at friends' houses, when their parents were out. During 1970 I went to fourteen house parties hosted by ten different people. It was an almost equal split between the girls and the lads with the Saltleyy girls hosting five parties, and the Ford brothers responsible for four of them. Parties at the Ford house involved the usual performance of up to thirty or forty people lingering on one set of steps waiting for Mr and Mrs Ford to exit via the set of steps at the other end of the building. Just above the excited chatter could be heard the familiar clanging of the casing of Party Sevens on the walls. The actual amount of alcohol consumed was not great as we had little money and not that much time as their mum and dad would return from the pub after closing. One or two did tend to "go for it". At one of the "Ford" parties the stair handrail was pulled from the wall when it failed to prevent the fall of Bernie Wright who was both incredibly strong and liked a drink. He was in the year above and went on to play professional football for Everton amongst others via Walasll FC.

My interest at the early parties seemed to be distracted by the venue rather than the event:

Saturday 28.02. 1970…."*Party at Ann's (*another Saltley girl*), good. Nice bungalow, very modern. 26 people 1/2 pt"*

As the year went on the numbers grew with forty-five party goers at Mark's in May, and at his brother Paul's 18th in October there were over fifty of us. Which was about the limit for the duplex.

PUBS DISCOVERED

At the end of May Mum and I were taken on holiday to Abersoch by the Muddimans (Uncle Peter and Auntie Hilda) along with their two youngest children Andrew (aged about eleven) and Julia (she was fifteen going on twenty!). I had a bit of a thing about Julia at the time but although a year younger than me she seemed older and out of reach. However, by the Friday (28th May) Julia suggested I take her to the "in" place in Abersoch at the time The White House. It was just a drink, two pints for me BUT my very first purchase of alcohol on licensed premises. A definite first.

Two weeks later I had my first pint in the pub that I have frequented more than any other pub..... The Ring O' Bells on Church Road, Yardley. 'O' levels started for most of my year on 1st June, the day after we returned from Abersoch, but mine started with English on the 9th. Following the Maths exam on the 15th, Mark and I ventured up to the "Ringers" for a 'well deserved' reward!

Monday 15.06. 1970.... *"Maths 1, NOT TOO BAD. Mark came up and played football. Had a drink at R.O.Bells 2pts".*

Not quite sure why we chose the Ringers but it was the nearest pub to the park. It would be the first of literally hundreds of visits to this pub, which has now been demolished to make way for some quite nice houses. Was Julia partly responsible for kick starting the frequenting of pubs and for distracting me from 'O' Level revision immediately before the exams? Of course not. Not surprisingly the next pub tested was the Makadown as it was very close to school. A very ordinary drinking establishment when first visited:

Saturday 11.07. 1970.... *"Went to the Mackadown with John L, (plus 3 great lads from my year) Harry (Asif Hussain), Tinker (Graham Murray), Dek (Derek Savage). Good laugh even though Mark (Ford) was missing. Met Gaz, Tez and*

Shrimp (Paul Wells) on their way back from a BL disco they said Elaine was upset".

More evidence of not paying Elaine enough attention probably due to the new pub experience. By the time I next went in the Mackadown (30th December 1970) it had been transformed into the "Gay Paris" which was very trendy for 1970.

In August John L and I discovered a new pub in the centre of Birmingham near New Street Station, called the Alhambra, and we loved it;

Saturday 08.08 1970….*"Went to last day at work. Went to the Alhambra with John it was fantastic. Also went to the Costermonger, alright. 2pts".*

It was just so different to the drinking pubs of Birmingham as it was lively, crowded and playing loud music. Being below stairs made it even more atmospheric. I went there a further eleven times before the year was out. Pub of the year! Amazing to go the three miles into town by bus, have only one or two drinks and return by bus sometimes on a school night!

POPPING ROUND TO MOTHERS

Prior to 1970 my interest in music was pretty main stream ie Beatles, Gerry and the Pacemakers, Hollies etc. Dad bought a well worn record player from a colleague at work, partly due to being "blackmailed" by my purchase of the Beatles "Can't buy me love" in 1964 with nothing to play it on.

Mark Ford and his brother Paul introduced me to Free at their first party in the January and my interest in progressive (Prog) rock was born. At the same time as Prog rock was flourishing the "skinheads" were bopping along to reggae which I was exposed to at Burney Lane youth club and I have to confess to purchasing Tighten Up Vol 2, but it didn't last. April saw the purchase of The Moody Blues "On the Threshold of a Dream" but the big break through was attending my first gig in July:

Friday 10.07. 1970. ...."*At night went to MOTHERS with Mark, good, saw Gentle Giant. 1pt.*

The club was situated above an inconspicuous furniture shop in the high street of the Birmingham suburb of Erdington about five miles from home along the number eleven bus route. It was Mark who introduced me to Mothers. He was taller and looked older than his years plus he had the advantage of an older brother who was into rock music.

From August 1968 to its closure in January 1971, MOTHERS was the venue for many famous rock bands. The Who, Fleetwood Mac, Led Zeppelin, Black Sabbath, Deep Purple, Family, Free and many more appeared in what the late DJ John Peel described as "the best club in Britain". Pink Floyd recorded half of their LP Ummagumma there in April 1969.

Nine days after my first visit I was back at MOTHERS this time with Brian to see Brett Marvin and the Thunderbolts who I described as "*enjoyable*". Mark was on holiday but Brian was, and still is, a massive music fan and even though a couple of years' younger was a big influence on my early musical appreciation.

The third and final visit to MOTHERS was on the 9th August to see Eric Clapton's recently formed band "Derek and the Dominoes";

Sunday 09.08.1970...."*Derek and the Dominoes featuring Eric Clapton - good band. Julia at MOTHERS.*

I remember bumping into Julia on the stairs but as the venue was packed and extremely hot we didn't stop to talk. It was so hot in fact that the band went off stage for a while to recover. I just about said hello to Julia who I think was with a chap who looked about ten years older than me. He was probably only about eighteen, but I knew my place. Although I didn't go to MOTHERS again this definitely started my love of going to see live bands, a past time that was to gather pace over the coming months.

The live gig bug had bitten and the first of many bands seen at Birmingham's Town hall were Procol Harum and Jethro Tull on 25th September. The former described in my diary as "*brilliant*" whereas 'Tull' were "*not so good*". No record of who went with me although I'm sure I didn't go alone. Next up were Taste (featuring Rory Gallagher), Stone the Crows (Maggie Bell), and Jake Holmes. I went with Bill from the Co-op restaurant, and some of his friends. No review recorded but my recollection was that it was "ok". By this time, I was really into the band Free and excited at the prospect of seeing them live at the Town Hall supported by Mott the Hoople on 6th October; "*both brilliant*". Not sure who I went with but almost certainly Mark and his brother Paul would have been there.

Luckily I am a hoarder, a habit which started early so I still have my ticket stubs to most of the gigs. The prices back then were incredibly good value. The Taste gig was eight shillings (40p) as were Procol Harum with Jethro Tull. The price rocketed to ten shillings (50p) for Free and Mott the Hoople. A couple of years ago I paid over £100 to see Fleetwood Mac. True the sound quality and seating has improved but what value back then! To put those prices into context the average ticket price was less than half the price of an album. Now that is value.

I started to buy albums both new, such as "Full Cream", 19/11 (call it a pound) and secondhand "Black Sabbath", 1/6 (8pish). The latter was bought from Ann the sister of my friend Tez. Even though the first track was missing I still loved it. It looked as though someone had taken a bite out of the edge. This meant careful placing of the needle, but it was still recorded in my diary as "*brilliant*". I only recently discovered that Ann, who is a couple of years older, was also a regular visitor to the MOTHERS club.

The singles charts in 1970 had an interesting mix of number ones. From the sublime "Bridge Over Troubled Water" (three weeks) to the ridiculous "Back Home" (three weeks) from the England football squad who were of course soon, ….'Back Home' (albeit unluckily). The number ones with the most personal connections were Edison Lighthouse's "Love grows where my Rosemary goes" (five weeks) and Norman Greenbaum's "Spirit in the Sky" (two weeks). The latter brings back memories of freaking out at Rowlands Road youth club and the former happy times at the BRS discos. Jimi Hendrix secured one week at number one following his death in September:

Thursday 19.11.1970….*"watched Top of the Pops - terrible. but Jimi Hendrix number one - great".*

GOING DOWN TO RIO

About 200 yards or so from my home stood the Yew Tree pub. Not a salubrious establishment, more a drinker's pub for passing trade on the intersection of several bus routes; the number 11 (outer circle), 15, 17, and 68.

It did however have a function suite named the RIO GRANDE. The "Rio" was a modern extension to the pub that up until mid 1970 ran a very boppy Sunday night dance called the Rio Grande Sunday Club. School friend Graham Buckley had tried to persuade me to try it and we even had an aborted attempt when I bottled out of the queue. But by September it had changed its musical direction to catch the Prog' rock wave. Sabbath Rock at the Rio was born (to be wild). How lucky I was living so close to a Prog Rock disco where we could all freak out to our hearts content and sweat for England!

My first visit was on Sunday 20th September. At first it was just Mark and I but this soon expanded with the usual suspects joining i.e. John L, Gaz etc. The DJ played all the latest popular rock music from the likes of Free, Family,

Atomic Rooster, Steppenwolf, Nice, plus more mainstream artists like Rod Stewart and the Rolling Stones. Lads could now "dance" on their own or with others, we were free to "freak" .... and we did!

As Christmas approached I bought two tickets for the Rio's Xmas Eve Party night and it was a great success:

Thursday 24.12.1970...."*Went to work, good, had champers and white wine (Co-op restaurant). Went to RIO— great. Gaz won champers and had two glasses. Gaz with Fiona, Mark, Yvonne.*"

NOT GOING OUT

I didn't spend too much time at home during the year. My diary reveals that just over 200 of the evenings were spent "out". This does not include many nights round at friends playing board games, cards or just listening to records. Also not counted are many nights playing football when the light allowed or going to football training at indoor venues. Of course nights spent revising should have taken up more than they did. As the year progressed my nights in fell from a high of twenty-four of the thirty-one in January to a low of just ten in December. Beer consumption followed the increase in nights out but was still fairly modest with the total number of pints drunk in the year just reaching ninety with nineteen downed in December alone. There were only eight pints quaffed at parties before my first purchase in Abersoch with Julia in June.

The board games were at this point still old favourites such as Monopoly and Totopoly. Wembley the knock out football game also made regular appearances. However, card games started to become more evident as money was now on the table. Not large amounts, "*up 2s4d*", but we were on a path that we would tread further in the future. Brag, the three card version, was the preferred game and we loved it. Strictly speaking,

Subbuteo was not a board game as the football game came with a cloth pitch to be placed on any flat surface before the twenty-two tiny plastic players were flicked to hit the ball. In the Duffin household it was different in that my brother Steve made an excellent job of attaching the cloth pitch to a piece of hardboard with an old bed sheet in between. It could therefore be classed as a board game. It was fun to play but it did lead to many heated disputes. I was often accused of pushing rather than flicking the players. I have to admit I was a "pusher".

When I was at home and not washing my hair, which was a necessity as the fashion meant longer locks which needed looking after, I often watched television. Like most people we had not yet moved to colour and certainly could not afford to for some time. There were some old favourites on the black and white box such as "Morecambe and Wise", which I described as "*brilliant*" on at least one occasion. "Top of the Pops" was essential viewing even when "Wandering Star" was at number one (3rd to 23rd March). Although now considered non-PC I seemed to enjoy Benny Hill, but I was sixteen. When it came to children's programmes I took to "Timeslip", which saw two teenagers, Simon and Liz, slipping through time. I had bit of a crush on Liz who was meant to be fifteen but I have recently discovered she was eighteen when it started this year.

There were new dramas in March including "Callan" and the unnerving "Doomwatch" which I loved, even the episode with the human eating rats. In earlier years I enjoyed the Gerry and Silvia Anderson programmes such as "Captain Scarlett" and "Thunderbirds" and was excited to welcome a new venture "UFO"; a more adult puppet-less series based on alien invasion. It didn't really take off but did lead to "Space 1999", which apart from being too optimistic about the date it was a marked improvement on "UFO".

One drama that I enjoyed was the legal series "The Main Chance" starring John Stride as the leading character David

Main. It ran for four series from 1969 to 1975. Little did I know it at the time but this series was to be a significant influence on my future.

When it came to comedy apart from the family fun of "Morecambe and Wise" there was "Please Sir" starring John Alderton, which appealed as I was still at school, despite the fact that the pupils appeared to be considerably older than the ones I shared a classroom with. However, my comedy focus was more radio based. My favourite was "I'm Sorry I'll Read That Again". Starring John Cleese, Tim Brooke-Taylor, Graeme Garden, David Hatch, Jo Kendall and Bill Oddie. It began just as I was starting Grammar school and finished just after I left. My brother and I would listen with pen in hand poised to capture all the best puns and jokes. I also listened to "the Navy Lark" which made Leslie Phillips and Jon Pertwee household names. It ran from just before I was born (1953) to a final 11th series in 1975. There were many repeats all of them featuring Leslie Phillips smoothly saying "a touch of the old left hand down a bit". Radio comedy shows such as these and classics like 'Hancock" and the "Goons" certainly help shape my sense of humour for better or worse!

SCHOOLS OUT (and back in again)

The outcome of my poor mock 'O' levels results should have been a new, more focused approach to schoolwork. Sadly not. Probably due to a number of factors the main one being my consistent and persistently over optimistic view of my ability to come good when it really mattered. The school's reaction was to remove me from the French and Physics exams to "avoid wasting the rate payers' money". This left; English, Math's, Geography, Geology, and my favourite, History. I had achieved close to the pass mark in all of these except Geology (34%) and I needed to pass just 4 to get into 6th Form. No problem!

The mocks finished mid January and we returned to school on the twenty-first. It is interesting to see from my diary that there were not many days spent at school before the actual 'O' levels started on the 1st June. During this eighteen-week period we suffered several days when the school was closed. First due to heavy snow and then a series of teacher's strikes. Add to this school holidays for half term, Easter and Whitsun and there I have my excuses in first even though I have to admit they do look pretty lame.

I knew that revision was required. However, revision implies that the subject matter has been learnt in the first place. Undeterred, I set to work about six weeks before the exams:

Monday 20.04.1970....."*stayed in and revised Geog and also watched television*"

My revision hours were up on the mocks but still way below the necessary levels;

Geography	16hrs
History	15.5hrs
Geology	9.5hrs
Maths	4hrs
English	4hrs
Unspecified	16hrs

Amazingly the week before the 'O' levels commenced Mum and I went on holiday to Abersoch with the Muddimans. Did I take any books? I think you know the answer. Diary says..... NO.

Interesting diary comments on the day of the exams;

Tuesday 09.06.1970..... *"English exam. Not TO bad!"* (note spelling)

Friday 12.06.1970......."*History, NOT TOO BAD, wrote ten sides but had headache. Geology paper HARD.*

The results came out in August while Mum and I were staying with my aunt and uncle in the Isle of Man. My brother Steve sent a telegram breaking the news:

Thursday 27.06.1970......*"Went to Douglas with Mum on the bus. Telegram two O levels English and Geog. Sunniest place in GB 12.01hrs"*

Well at least the sun was shinning and I didn't seem too upset or surprised. A week later I was back at school to be interviewed about my options. The outcome was fairly predictable, i.e. another shot at the 'O' levels with the addition of two new subjects, English Literature and British Constitution. I was happy with this but surprised by the insistence that Physics was included which had previously been dropped after the mocks to "avoid wasting rate payers' money". There was also some chatter following the revelation that only five out of forty had passed History. I had come tenth in the mocks and should have passed. Today there would be an "inquest" and papers possibly re-marked. In 1970 we just moaned and said to each other that this just proved what a poor teacher Taffy Thomas was! I immediately decided to re-take the ones I failed at the next opportunity which was in the coming January, confident of success as usual.

The main playground was almost entirely devoted to games of football at break time. It was surrounded on three sides by grass, which was out of bounds. There was a six-foot wire fence on one side separating our boys school from Byng Kendrick girl's school. We were not allowed to go to the fence to talk to the girls with detention the usual punishment if caught. However, one lunchtime in the summer a small group of fellow 5th formers bravely ignored the threat and began excitedly chatting to a small group of girls. After a few minutes the girls enthusiastically pointed across the busy playground and instructed the lads to immediately bring that good-looking boy over to them. The next thing I knew I was lifted off my feet, removed from the football and carried unceremoniously over to the girls. But before I could make sense of the situation I heard the girls shriek in unison; "no, not him, that one". I was dumped in more ways than one and walked sheepishly back to the game. I cannot recall who the good looking one was as I was not the least bit interested.

MORE TO SCHOOL THAN EXAMS

I enjoyed school life. From the first year I had thrown myself in whole-heartedly. In sport, I captained the cricket team where I opened the bating. Played hooker in the rugby team and later played regularly in the basketball team despite not yet growing to any real height.

I was selected for the choir and sang solos at the Christmas carol concerts in both 1965 and 1966. They were nerve racking events causing me to leave the stage not long before I was due to sing "See Amid the Winters Snow" for a quick visit to the (fortunately) nearby boys room. I enjoyed performing too, especially the Coventry Carol where I was accompanied by a guitarist called King but can't recall his first name.

Comic operas were next on the musical agenda following the arrival of a new music teacher, Mr T R Sandland (nick named Tressy after a doll!) who had different ideas to his predecessor Mr Jones (Jonah). He was heavily influenced towards comic opera by Mr Hutton (known as Crut, no idea where that came from). The first of the three Gilbert and Sullivan operas we were to perform was Trial By Jury in 1968. A relatively short comic opera, probably chosen as an experiment to see if we could pull it off and also see what the audience reaction would be. A real trial! I was one of the 'women' in the public gallery as all the parts were played by the pupils at our all boys' school. On other occasions, we would sometimes invite the girls from the next-door girls' school Byng Kendrick to take part, but not this time.

The funniest memory I have is during one of the rehearsals the boy singing the line "I have one word my lord and that is rapture" changed the ending to "RUPTURE". Predictably there was uproar at the time and from then on there was also a great deal of control required every time it reached the rupture point. However, it went very well and amazingly we "girls" did not suffer any flak from our peers.

Next up was Pirates of Penzance (1969). No cross dressing here as I was cast as a butch pirate. Well, a pirate any way. I have two memories from "Pirates". First was in the dress rehearsal where my sword got stuck into the stage floor. I professed it was an accident but I am not so sure. The other was that one of my fellow pirates was played by a boy from a lower year, one Kevin McNally, now a well-known actor made famous through his role as the first mate Joshamee Gibbs in all of the Pirates of the Caribbean films. How bizarre that he is now making a very good living from being a pirate again.

In the late 1990's my wife Sue and I were invited to the Laurence Olivier awards in London by American Express who were the sponsors. It was a great night particularly because the sponsor's table was situated in the middle of a room full of actors. I quickly looked through the programme and was delighted to find Kevin sat with his wife (Phyllis Logan of Lovejoy and Downton Abbey fame). As soon as the official proceedings finished I found their table and somewhat hesitantly approached Kevin and asked him if he remembered our performance in" Pirates". He literally jumped to his feet, put an arm around my shoulder and we were straight into "with cat like tread". What a performance from the man who has been in everything from Dr Who to Hamlet and from Spice World to Supernatural. Of course, it was late on and we had both had a drop or two but it doesn't really matter whether he remembered me or not, it was a memorable night for me.

HMS Pinafore was my final G&S. This time I played a sailor. More great fun.

I continued in the choir and can recall performing St Nicholas at St Peters in Saltley where Kevin Knight, who had an outstanding voice, excelled. I also took part in several school plays, mostly as an extra in crowd scenes. These included Captain Scuffleboom a one act play, and The Devils Disciple. When rehearsing for the latter we (the crowd) were asked to make more noise and the usual "rhubarb, rhubarb" was suggested but we took the direction too literally and a rather disturbing rhubarb chant ensued.

There are of course good and bad teachers in every school. It may be due to my memory or my academic performance but I cannot recall too many good ones at CGS. The pick of the 1965 to 1971 crop were Hutton, Sellis, Jones (M) and Walker and possibly Wakeley. Mr Hutton (Crut) was top of my list. He was my form teacher in the first year (1P) and taught me Geography in my 'O' level year. It is no coincidence that on my first attempt at the 'O' levels this was my best result, grade C, the second highest pass grade of A, C, E that the London Board awarded. He was also heavily involved in both the sport (cricket and rugby) and music life of the school. He had no problem controlling classes with quite a strict approach but at the same time he was quick to appreciate a joke. In my first year report he made an interesting point; "A pleasant likeable boy. He must ensure that his high spirits can not be taken for misbehaviour". How true. I did not realise at the time how young he was partly due to the wearing of what looked like demob suits. He was only in his twenties. He taught using an overhead projector and issuing copies of information. Far better than those who scribbled endlessly on the blackboard for us to slavishly copy.

Mr Hutton (Brian) still lives in Yardley close to where I was brought up. I have visited him twice, once in 1974 when I was thinking of becoming a PE teacher, and more recently in 2013 with fellow pupil John Roden who at the time lived just a couple of roads away. It was a very enjoyable reunion. I was so pleased to be able to tell him how much I respected him and how he helped shape my future. I was able to inform him that his prediction that I would make an excellent trade union negotiator did not thankfully materialize. Nor did becoming a PE teacher.

Mr Sellis was another fairly young chap. Not much humour here but he took time to explain various mathematical complexities. Math's was the only subject I ever came top in, admittedly in the first year before the subject became a little more challenging. Mr Jones became my fourth year form teacher. He took a common sense approach and was most helpful and sympathetic when my Dad died in the February.

Mr Walker took me for English in the third year and was also heavily involved in the school plays. There are two events that stand out. In an end of year English exam, we were asked to define the word "cliché or was it clique". It doesn't really matter, the point was that he came up to me and said I was the only person in the whole year (90 pupils) to get it right. I was mystified as I had no recollection of it and was pretty sure it wasn't me. I stayed quiet and took the credit! The other was much later when I had decided not to stay on for 'A' levels. He stopped me in the corridor and spent a good few minutes trying to persuade me to take English at 'A' level. I was touched particularly as he hadn't taught me for a couple of years.

The teacher on the edge of making the "best" list was Mr Wakeley. He was my second year form teacher who also taught me English. He was young, enthusiastic and even dared to wear polo neck jumpers and no gown. Along with Mr Walker he was also heavily involved with the school plays. On a school skiing trip to Austria he broke his right leg and was absent for quite a while. But he never lost his writing talent as he demonstrated on my school report; "the chief clown is seldom top of the form". I wasn't!

At the other end of the spectrum were a few candidates but I will only mention one. Mr May (known as Pip) was deputy head for many years. He had been at the school since 1930 so he was probably on the glide path to retirement by the time we "crossed swords" in my fourth year English set. A couple events stand out. The first was his love of H G Wells' "History of Mr Polly". I now appreciate it was meant to be ironic but May failed to explain to sceptical fourth year pupils the value of this work. I never had a problem with English as a subject but did find his old-fashioned approach difficult to adapt to.

The other was a good example of my "high spirits' and his total lack of a sense of humour. He was explaining to the class how towards the end of the war there was an experiment where small pieces of thin metal were dropped out of airplanes to prevent the enemy's radar working effectively. Young Duffin asks, "Sir, was this done to FOIL the enemy". The class was amused, but he was not. I was ordered to leave the room and stand outside. He also announced in assembly that he was fed up with the damage caused by the increasing number of football games in the playground. Action was required and he was taking it: "forthwith there is a ban on imitation plastic footballs". I stood there pondering whether to ask what imitation plastic was but decided to be sensible for once. It didn't last.

I was heavily involved in the sporting side of the school. Cricket was my main interest that came from my Dad who was a useful cricketer playing for the Co-op alongside his best friend Peter Muddiman (Uncle Peter). He was ambidextrous a skill he used most notably in tennis where he served with one hand and played his ground strokes with the other. After winning one tennis competition he attempted to hurdle the net in celebration but fell and broke his arm. He was clearly trying to relive the days when he represented the RAF in the high jump whilst serving in Egypt during the war.

I spent many happy hours playing cricket in the drive with my brother Steve. The gap between our house and the

Beresfords next door led to the development of a reasonably stylish straight drive but few other attacking shots. Driving past the end of the houses into the road was rewarded with 2. To secure a 4 the tennis ball had to reach the wall of the house opposite occupied by Reg and Mary Tranter and their children Mark and Gaynor.

Before starting at Central GS I had played for my junior school Hobmoor from the age of nine. Such an early introduction to competitive school cricket was due to two main factors, the ability to bowl overarm, and the very limited number of boys to choose from. We only had one class per year and, strangely, a disproportionately high number of girls. I was captain in the last year and opened the bowling and batting. If you could bowl overarm and straight you took wickets. I still have the scorebook (actually a City of Birmingham Education Committee exercise book). It records my bowling for the 1965 season as 49 overs 16 maidens 22 wickets and 85 runs. On the batting side I had 3 top scores as well as 3 successive ducks.

At Central I completely lost the ability to bowl but my batting progressed. I captained the side and opened the batting. My main opening partner was Keith Florey (Floss) a very capable all round sportsman. We were an ideal opening pair as we were complete opposites. Keith was an attacking left hander who played predominately off the back foot. I was a right handed bat favouring the front foot with a straight bat (think of a young Chris Tavare or any blocker). We broke a number of school records mainly due to Keith's accumulation of runs plus my ability to just stay there.

As the years progressed my visual deficiencies caused by the late detection of a squint in my right eye and the development of short sightedness in my left eye began to affect my ability to pick up the ball as the pace increased. This was evidenced when I was chosen to represent Mr Davidson's X1 against the first team. The fast bowler was Bernie Wright (later to play professional football for Everton and others). He was a powerfully built lad who was rumoured to have won the Birmingham schools shot put competition without getting changed! I saw him running up to the wicket and the next thing I knew was a searing pain in my solar plexus and being unable to breathe. I was helped off the pitch and slowly recovered but his mark stayed for many days.

By 1970 I was in the second team and managed to score a few runs. Amazingly I was selected for a 6-a-side completion at the old Centrals ground but we were knocked out quite early on. I went straight to Elaine's to watch England's unlucky defeat to Brazil. I still remember Bank's save shown in glorious colour, excellent!

A couple of weeks later I managed my best ever score, thirty-eight against Saltley on the 20th June. This must have impressed the first team selectors as I was immediately elevated to the first team to play the Old Boys the very next day. I am not sure whether my selection was down to my runs or the fact that the next day was the World Cup final reducing availability. My diary does not record my score, which probably means a duck. Never mind, off I went to Elaine's to watch the World Cup Final in colour. Brazil 4 Italy 1.

I was not so keen on rugby but played for the school in the 2nd and 3rd years as hooker. The school was extremely fortunate to have two England rugby internationals as teachers, Colin McFadyean and Sam Doble. When they joined in 1965 they were twenty-two and twenty-one years of age and both played club rugby for Moseley who were a top side in those days.

McFadyean took me for history and Doble for PE. I found Doble a difficult young man who was quite hard on poor performers. He was unsympathetic to those whose bodies did not find it easy to adapt to the challenges of basic gymnastics. He seemed to enjoy making some of the larger boys hang from the wall bars as punishment. To be kind I will put it down to youth, but we did not get on. I didn't really have the physique for rugby but had pretty good handling and ball skills and was a reasonable tackler. As the lads all got bigger and I didn't I retreated from playing to working on Saturdays at the Co-op.

One of the good things about school basketball was that the matches were played in the week, often on a Friday after school. Although not tall I had ball sense and was keen. Our teacher Mr Weightman had I think played the sport at a high level. I made the squad regularly from the 3rd year onwards and usually was in the game at some point although my appearances were restricted to right attack, due to lack of inches. But I enjoyed it and still played into my 50's but only for fun. Eventually reaching five feet ten inches tall I was certainly no magic Johnson, more like Boris Johnson!

SPORT OUTSIDE SCHOOL

For as long as I can remember I was always kicking or catching a ball. My Dad's love of sport was a big factor and he was keen to spend time with Steve and I catching the ball in the garden. I had played in the primary school football team in the last two school years. Usually "up front" but at that age we all wanted to be the centre forward which often resulted in all ten outfield players rushing forward en masse. Poor old Mr Hughes, our teacher, patrolled the touch line trying to establish some sense of order into our play. He usually failed, as did the team.

Central Grammar was a rugby school with soccer restricted to the playground. However, 1970 saw my return to organised football, Graham Murray (in those non-pc days affectionately known as Tinker) invited some of us to join the team he played for, Royal Star. As previously established I was not very tall and definitely on the skinny side (*9 st 3 lbs*) therefore I should not have been surprised to be selected for the first game of the season at right back. But I was! Mark (Ford) was chosen at wing half (midfield) and Tinker right wing;

Sunday 13.09.1970…. *"played football at right back. Lost 8-2. I played well. 3-0 at halftime".*

I played through the rest of the year even managing to win six of our 16 matches up to Christmas. But still at right back! However, I kept my place unlike Mark who was dropped after the first 3 matches and replaced by his pal "Gibbo" Dowson. We met for practice on Thursday evening at the boys club in Shard End followed by team selection at the Raven pub. On the 29th October we held a vote for captain at which I managed to secure one vote (probably mine).

Many hours were spent kicking a ball with the local lads either "up the field" (Marlborough cricket ground) which some of the houses on our square backed on to, or one of the municipal parks nearby (the Oaklands, Yardley Old Park, Queens Road Park or Gilbertstone). We were well off for parks ands they were all just a short walk from home.

Apart from playing football I was also keen to follow the Villa. Aston Villa was in the blood as both my grandfather and father were fans. My Dad was a season ticket holder in the Witton Lane stand for as long as I can remember. My uncle Cyril (Mum's sister Joyce's husband) had a season ticket in the Trinity Road stand. My first match was Villa versus Nottingham Forest on the 23rd April 1962. I was 7 and a half. Dad took me and my friend Peter Seeny from just around the corner to the open Witton end and met us at the exit at the end. Villa won 5-1. They ended that season comfortably mid table in the top division. In 1970 my visits to Villa Park were limited by my Saturday jobs but I still managed to attend 8 games. Villa were relegated at the end of the 69/70 season to the 3rd division their lowest ever position. But things picked up later in the year with the highlight a league cup semi final victory over a Manchester United side that included Best, Law and Charlton. My diary records:

Weds 23.12.1970….. *"went to Villa- brilliant. Villa 2 (Lockhead and McMahon) Man Utd 1 (Kidd). Now in final Feb 27th – Going"!*

I went to that semi final with John L and his dad, Arthur. Nearly 60,000 attending and experiencing a truly memorable victory. I also went to the Blues earlier in the year when they played West Bromwich Albion accompanied by Gaz, Brian and surprisingly Paul Wells (not a big footie fan).

GET YOUR "FLICKS" FOR FREE

John L's mum Doreen was a real character who I got on with well. In 1970 she had a part time job at the ABC New Street on the ticket desk. A real plus for John and I was that Doreen benefitted from a free pass that we were only too happy to use regularly. During the year, I went to the cinema twenty-three times. The free pass was used thirteen times. For the other ten I took Elaine five times and the remaining five were with a mix of the usual suspects.

There were some classics films such as Butch Cassidy and the Sundance Kid, Bonny and Clyde, and Bullet. Elaine and I saw Easy Rider twice in one week not due to its quality but to the late cancellation of a Burney Lane disco just down the road from where the film was playing (the Rock). I can also admit to seeing The Sound of Music on a free pass at the Scala Cinema where Doreen worked before moving to the ABC New St. Less notable films but enjoyed all the same were: Spring and Port Wine starring James Mason and Carry On Up The Jungle. Both of which were with Elaine. The Carry On film was screened at the Odeon New Street where I went completely mad and bought two top price ten shilling seats from my first week's wages at the Co-op restaurant. I knew how to show her a good time.

PUPPY LOVE CONTINUES

Our first disagreement at the end of June did not lead to an immediate separation although there was a second wobble just two days later:

Sunday 28.06.1970......."*went to Marks with Elaine, Gaz and Bri but too many people all boys. Treated Elaine terribly. Forgot to kiss her goodnight. Must apologise*".

Being conscientious I did, the next day. Yes, we were only kids but we got on well most of the time and spent quite a large part of 1970 together.

Intelligent, attractive and having a good sense of humour meant Elaine was great company and put up with the almost constant accompaniment of my mates. But by July it was me, not Elaine who became a little restless. Elaine had a phone installed on the 24th July meaning there was no way of avoiding her. We were still seeing a lot of each other with trips to the cinema to see "Planet of the Apes", "Hells Angles 69", "Butch Cassidy and the Sundance Kid". We were still going to Burney Lane and visits to her home were also fairly frequent, not to mention the odd house party. However, towards the end of August Gary told me something that changed my relationship with Elaine:

Thursday 13.08.1970....."*Gaz told me Ann Jackson wanted to go out with me. Decided definitely to pack in Elaine. So try at Yvonne's party on Saturday*".

Saturday 15.08.1970...... "*Joy's wedding*". (This was Joy Beresford from next door and was the first outing for my very first suit, it was bottle green!). *"Went to party at Yvonne's. PACKED. Elaine in. Words to Elaine* (on extra page in diary) *"let's get a few things straight, Carol was not true'* (don't remember this!) *"and I am sorry I did not speak tonight. But it* *had to end sometime didn't it? I have been treating you rotten and it would only get worse wouldn't it?"*

"Snogged with Fiona, Elaine Smith and Ann. Took Ann home. Ann said in 3 weeks' time she would go out with me if she was not seeing anyone else. Kissed with Ann for some time. She has my tie."

Next day:

Sunday 16.08.1970.......*"Stayed in and phoned Ann to try to get my tie back. Dossed at night nothing much doing at all".*

Dramatic or what! I would like to say it was Gary's fault for telling me of Ann's interest but I think it was just time to move on, albeit not very far as Ann was a friend both in and out of school.

The very next day I was off to the Isle of Man with my Mum via a rough sea crossing from Liverpool. Ann must have found someone else or thought better of her promise as the diary is silent on the outcome. No mention of Ann, or for that matter, my tie. However, the split with Elaine was the start of a new phase kicked off with a return to school to resit my 'O' levels. The next few weeks saw the discovery of the Alhambra and other pubs. Also the Rio became a regular haunt plus more gigs. Add to this regular football and it becomes evident that I had clearly moved on and Elaine was history.

Well not quite:

Saturday 26.09.1970....... *"Mark F is now going out with Elaine J. Went to the Parisian with Buck* (school friend Graham Buckley), *John L, Arry (Asif Hussain). Met Mark, Elaine, Fiona and Mrag"*

There were clearly no hard feelings as the next evening Mark *"bought me a pint"* at the Rio. Mark only saw Elaine a couple of times and our friendship was undamaged.

Two days later I was in a reflective mood:

Tuesday 29.09.1970……. *"Mark, Gibbo and John L came over to my house. Played records and talked about the past"*

Well I had just turned seventeen so there was much to reflect on! But the most obvious advantage of reaching such an age was the ability to learn to drive. We had kept my dad's Austin A40 for my brother Steve to drive. Unfortunately learning to drive didn't start well:

Sunday 11.10.1970…….. *"first driving lesson but Steve told off by policeman"*

Can't recall exactly what happened but Steve was not happy. My second and final lesson from my brother ended when the car broke down for which I got the blame. Not long after that the car was sold to a scrap dealer. However, a visit from the local constabulary shortly after informed us that it had been used in a robbery. I could not imagine it being used as a get away vehicle. My driving lessons were put on hold until I started work and could afford to pay for "proper" ones.

Back at school the middle of October saw a school dance. Predictably the Saltley girls were there and yes less than two months after our split we were back together:

Tuesday 20.10.1970……. *"going out again with Elaine. Met her at the school dance. –Pegasus played, good. Had a chat with Donavon's brother".* (Donavon was an English teacher and his brother was the drummer in the band).

Mark and Paul Ford were born only one year apart and their seventeenth and eighteenth birthdays were at the end of October. Things must have been going well with Elaine as I walked her home from their joint party. Mark's was the more eventful party as Gaz finished with Yvonne and John L had 8 pints and threw up. I had a half (no change there then).

My diary records that two days later "*Gaz came and we discussed things*" no record of what was discussed but there had been some sort of disagreement, which lead to Gaz and Brian going their own way for a while.

November saw more visits with Elaine to the Alhambra pub, and even Small Heath Fair. Steve Martin (year above and friend of Paul Ford) had his eighteenth party. Another one at the Smith's where all the lads got drunk and it was my turn to call for "Hughie" followed this.

As Christmas approached I took Elaine to the Rio for the first time where we exchanged gifts on Christmas eve and toasted each other with the champagne that Gaz had won.

Elaine doesn't get a mention in my diary, which is surprising as she gave me Gentle Giant's first album as a Xmas present that night, inspiringly called "Gentle Giant". I was delighted. When I saw Gentle Giant that July at Mothers they had only recently formed from Simon Dupree and the Big Sound who had a top ten hit with 'Kites' reaching number nine in 1967. I bought their next three albums always hoping that the magic of their debut album would be recaptured, sadly it never was. Their second album was called "Acquiring the Taste" but I never did. Looking back, it is easy to see how the excitement generated by experiencing my first live band and nightclub clouded my view of them.

Our final date of the year was on the 30th December when we went to the refurbished Mackadown Pub (now a Lidl supermarket).

The year ended as it began with the usual New Years Eve Party at the Yardley's. But what a difference a year makes!

CHAPTER 2 1971: All work but lots of play

On the world stage the Vietnam war grinds on and the space race between the two super powers, America and USSR, intensifies. Closer to home decimalisation comes into force; Rolls Royce declares bankruptcy; and a postal strike begins. The entertainment world sees the death of Jim Morrison, and Charles Manson is found guilty of the murder of Sharon Tate. In sport the first one day cricket international is played between England and Australia.

There is a familiar start to the year for me with a New Year's Eve party at Eileen and Gordon Yardley, the sister and brother-in-law of the Beresfords, our next-door neighbours at Vicarage Road, *"home at 2.30am"*

ELAINE....MAKE YOUR MIND UP TIME

Things started well with us meeting up on the second day of the New Year, although we were not alone:

Saturday 02.01.1971......*"tried to find a party with John L, Gaz and Elaine. Failed. Went to Elaine's with drink. Watched TV and saw that 66 people had been killed at the Ibrox football ground after a barrier collapsed"*.

Things then went pretty quiet for a week or two as I was, unusually for me, concentrating on revising for the upcoming 'O' level resits and mocks. However, during my extended study period, I still found time to call Elaine, watch football and go to a gig. All that studying must have affected my head as the phone calls to Elaine culminated in yet another ending:

Saturday 16.01.1971........*"Went down the Villa, won 1-0 v Port Vale. Packed Elaine in over the phone at 7.05pm. Went to the Alhambra"*.

However, the break up didn't last long. Three weeks later we met up at the school dance and I discovered some interesting information:

Tuesday 19.02.1971....."*School disco (3/-). Went with John L, Gaz and Gray (Graham Buckley). Elaine, Yvonne, Sue, Marg, Ann, Elaine S and Jane were there. Found out that Elaine had two-timed me 3 times –CHEEK - but Ann said Elaine missed me and would still go out with me*"

Well that was good enough for me and – surprise, surprise – four days later it was all back on again;

Saturday 13.02.1971........"*Rang Elaine and asked her to Paul Ford's party. Fiona and Yvonne also there. Post strike still on*"

Good to know that the rekindling with Elaine had not dampened my interest in current affairs. However, the party or Elaine or both can't have been all that good as the next day I was clearly having second thoughts. I rang Elaine to 'cancel' taking her to the Rio, but not wanting to miss out, I still went. This may have pricked my conscience as I recorded "*think I have boobed*!". By now I was clearly having third thoughts as four days later we were back on track. We went to her school dance, without incident, followed soon after by trips to the Parisian pub in town and to see a band at the Swan. Elaine's birthday was a couple of days later (25th Feb) and being a generous lad I sent her a card and a ticket to see 'Free' who were performing at the Town Hall the night before her birthday. I can't remember what I was wearing but Elaine dressed to impress wearing a "*new maxi skirt (cord)*". I rang her on her birthday and invited her to a party on the Saturday after I had returned from watching Villa in the League Cup final at Wembley.

However, just one week later and I was at it again. This was not good behaviour and my passion for "stats" at such a tumultuous time was inappropriate to say the least.

Saturday 07.03,1971......."*Packed ELAINE in over the phone.*

Spoke to her for fifty minutes trying to calm her down. (10 months, 1 week and 2 days or 309 days)".

ELAINE.....MOVING ON AND OFF

After the "ending" in March our paths crossed occasionally due to common friends and venues. I may have regretted my decision to end things as I clearly missed her at party time:

Saturday 03.04.1971....*"Party at Albert Fisher's (friend of Mark Ford's) ...Gaz and I bored. I missed Elaine a lot today"*

Things started to rekindle some months later in August. Not again I hear you cry! Two days after returning from Skegness and saying goodbye to Lynn (full details of the boys' holiday to follow under "it's fun to stay at the YMCA) we bumped into each other at the Barley Mow pub;

Monday 16.08.1971.....*"Went to the Barley Mow with Gaz, John L, Mark, Sweat, Bernie and mob. Elaine cried on my shoulder but I told her it was no good".*

Common sense prevailed for once as I was now involved with the very keen Lynn after our roller coaster week in Skeggy. We then had a near miss a couple of weeks later when after bumping into Elaine on the way from the Ringers Gaz, John L and arranged to go to her house the next day to play records;

Tuesday 31.08.1971.......*"took Acquiring the taste (new Gentle Giant album) and the Strawbs. Stayed until 4,15pm. I nearly got off with her".*

Close thing but still not together. Four days later the gang were at the Hideaway (I think this was at the Bulls Head near the Swan) to see the group Canyon. Gaz, John L, Bri and Shrimp (Paul Wells) went plus Yvonne and Elaine. As a result, we were back together. In self-defence although "technically" involved with Lynn it could not yet really be described as a relationship as it was still in it's infancy. Have you bought that? The next day I took Elaine to the Rio and even walked her home! Changed man? The following Friday I took Elaine into town;

Friday 10.09.1971....."*Took Elaine first to The Tavern and treated her to a BRANDY AND BABYCHAM, then on to ABC New Street on John's free pass to see Le Mans (Steve McQueen)*".

This date was unusual for a couple of reasons: it was just the two of us for a change; and I bought her a brandy and Babycham. That was really pushing the boat out! Well I had been paid that day and it we did have a free cinema pass. I am not sure whether Elaine was into motor racing, I certainly wasn't, but on the whole, this was a better performance from young Duffin. This could have been a case of trying to keep my options open with the Lynn situation being at such an early and uncertain stage, or maybe I just liked Elaine. I would like to think it was the latter.

We were out together again the next night at the Hideaway but this time it was a full turnout with the local boys which now included Paul W (AKA Shrimp) plus a couple of the Central boys and of course Elaine's best friends Yvonne and Fiona. Shame the group didn't turn up. Sunday night at the Rio would make it three nights on the trot. This was the night that I went around the block thinking that "Jagger" (full story later) was after me. It all ended well and I saw Elaine home, eventually. Monday night made it four nights running and was probably a record as we all turned up at the Barley Mow. We seemed to be back on at full strength but the northern lass (Lynn) was about to make an appearance for my 18th birthday four days later.

The day before my birthday and Lynn's arrival I phoned Elaine and spoke for half and hour but I did not make a note of the contents in my diary. She knew it was my 18th and we had just had four really good nights. How did I explain my unavailability on my special birthday? I then rang Lynn and had a five minute conversation.

The birthday weekend with Lynn must have been a success and I can only assume that after having such a good time I had decided to progress the relationship with Lynn, but unfortunately this meant that Elaine was once again about to be let down:

Monday 27.09.1971........"*Went to Barley Mow with Elaine, Gaz and Yvonne. Yvonne finished with Gaz and I finished with Elaine - for good. I feel free and unburdened*"

I think the overriding emotion was more likely to be guilt or at least it should have been. And it is not the first time we've heard "for good"! Not surprisingly with so many mutual friends our paths continued to cross as they did just over three weeks later at Paul Ford's 19th birthday on 23rd October;

Saturday 23.10.1971......"*Went to Sweat's party. Walked there and back, home at 12.25am. Good party. Elaine and I are just good friends. Lynn rang.*"

I have no idea what "*just good friends*" meant to me then. Perhaps we had moved to a new level where we just hooked up occasionally when it suited us both. There is some evidence to support this as we met up a few times before the end of the year, at my old school's dance (15th Dec) and the Curved air concert (17th Dec). We were certainly together at Yvonne's party (27th Dec), as I recorded "*getting off with Elaine*". But we will have to wait until the New Year to find out more.

SCHOOL - THE HARDER YOU WORK........

Repeating the 5th year was never going to be easy but I did seem to learn a lesson that would last a lifetime. Firstly, being positive and confident is useful but definitely no substitute for hard work. Secondly knowing how you want things to work out is a pretty good place to start.

I still had not really got over failing History, my favourite subject, the previous June. Now was my chance to put the record straight. The exam was scheduled for Thursday the 14th January. I started serious revision with three hours on New Year's Day and continued every day. I sat the exam and felt it went well:

Thursday 14.01.1971........"*History 'O' Level. NOT TOO BAD, wrote 15 sides*"

I also increased my revision for Geology and felt that exam was also "*not too bad*". Maths was split into three papers each of which had to be passed. I described one as being "hard" and my confidence was low. I seemed to do very little revision for maths, which I think, was due to the misconception that you couldn't really revise for it. I had to wait until the end of March for the results and there was a shock in store:

Wednesday 24.03.1971......"*Had exam results: Maths FAIL (F), knew it!; Geology FAIL (F), disappointing: History PASS (A) shocked*".

The History result was further evidence that the first result was at the very least suspicious. Going from an F to an A even with more work was quite a turn around.

There was more good news on the exam front with excellent results in the two new subjects. The mocks for these were taking place at the same time as the resit 'O' levels i.e. mid-January. I was determined to do well in both new subjects and put in much more work than last year. I came first in British Constitution with a clear 16% ahead of the second placed pupil who just happened to be my good friend from the year below, John L. I came second in English literature a subject I was enjoying. Bearing in mind those who sat these exams were not just my fellow resit pupils, but also the current 5th year they were results to be proud of.

The real exams were in June and all went well this time. Well nearly all. I was relieved to pass Maths and delighted to get the second highest grade in English Literature despite suffering a migraine during the exam. My only failure was Geology but six 'O' level passes of which four were passed at the first attempt was a distinct improvement.

THE MAIN CHANCE

The fall back job at last year's careers evening was the police force, as long as you were tall enough, which at that stage thankfully I wasn't. It was to be a very different interview this time. To stimulate discussion, I was asked which TV programmes I enjoyed. I mentioned "The Main Chance" starring John Stride as a solicitor whose life is transformed after moving from London to Leeds. The interview went well:

Wednesday 31.03.1971...."*He suggested that I become a legal executive after 5 years training*".

Added to this were other less interesting careers. The civil service and local authority both sounded pretty dull by comparison to a legal executive! Interviews soon followed. First up was the Law Society (28th April) where I was told; "*I should get the job*". They would arrange a couple of interviews with legal firms. The first firm was Needham and James (Mr James);

Monday 17.05.1971....."*toad type bloke. Asked daft questions and made me feel uneasy*".

Not sure what a "*toad bloke*" is but I was clearly not impressed and they probably weren't either. The next legal firm was Wragge & Co. A much larger practice (100+ people) situated in the same building as the other firm but occupying two floors;

Wednesday 09.06.1971......."*Interview at Wragge & Co. Went well. Saw Mr Whiting-Smith and Mr Liddle. Both friendly*".

The interviews at the Civil Service and Local Authority were both ok. The Civil Service asked me a couple of questions on current affairs, which I answered easily. Both offered me a job but I was not sufficiently impressed with either of them when the chance to becoming an 'executive' beckoned! Only two days after the interview at Wragges their offer arrived by post. I was "*pleased*". I was to attend a two week induction course at the Law Society for this year's intake of trainees. I was going to be an executive!

THE REAL WORK STARTS

Working at the Co-op over the last two years had paid dividends. Earning some money helped to take some financial pressure off my mum, and meant that I could watch a lot of bands, buy records and new clothes. Equally important were the "life skills" I picked up, such as how to work with people and adapt to different management styles. I was learning a tremendous amount without realising it at the time. After leaving school I continued to work at the Co-op restaurant in town until we went to Skegness in August. My career as a trainee legal executive was due to start on Monday 6th September with a two week course for new trainees run by the Law Society located in Temple Street just a couple of hundred yards from the Wragge & Co offices in Windsor House.

Day one saw about a dozen trainees settle down for films and lectures. It was immediately obvious that the age range was surprisingly wide with nine of the trainees being 18 or over and having completed 'A' levels and one chap, Bruce, probably in his early thirties. I think I was the youngest and probably least qualified which was surprising yet comforting. There were four of us from Wragges. John McCormack and Michael O'Mahoney had both joined from being police cadets and therefore knew each other. The other recruit was John Hunter who quickly became known as "Scout" because he always walked at least two paces in front of the rest of us.

The next few days provided a very good insight into the various branches of the law and work we could be involved in. We were taken on a visit to the Law Courts where I recognised one of the defendants being tried at the time. He was a well known local bad boy on trial for both rape and "doing over" the Post Office by Yardley parish church. We were also shown around the Magistrates Court and the local stock exchange. The stamp office was a place I would return to frequently over the coming months. This was where the duty (tax) was paid on legal documents such as conveyances with a stamp embossed as proof. During the second week we were introduced to the lecturer who would be taking us for Law each Tuesday as part of our day release (afternoon and evening) at Matthew Boulton College. He was instantly nicknamed "Spock" as he had an uncanny resemblance to Leonard Nimoy who played the character in Star Trek.

We had plenty of breaks and frequently took the opportunity to visit local pubs for lunch, mainly the Parisian but also the Gilded Cage and the Nelson. By the end of the fortnight we had a good understanding of what our training could entail .I also started to form friendships not only with the chaps from Wragges, but also with some of the other trainees particularly Paul, Dave and Bruce. Paul was working for Needham and James in our building (Windsor House). This was the firm I was interviewed for but didn't take to. The next week saw my first day at Wragges;

Monday 20.09.1971........."Started at 9.15am. I am working with an Articled Clerk called Jonathan Price. He is a helpful chap. I worked harder than I thought I would on my first day".

I think Jonathan was close to finishing his 'Articles' and becoming a qualified solicitor. The partner I reported to was John Duncombe (JHD) who turned out to be very serious, of slight build and a little old fashioned for a man in his 30's. His secretary Ann Taylor was great. She was very helpful, friendly, and in many ways quite protective towards young Duffin.

The way we were trained was interesting being a combination of "sitting with Nellie" or in my case Jonathan or DIY. There were about 17 partners in all and four in our work group, any of which could give you a file to work on. All JHD's files started with a 'P'. It was clear that most of my work would be conveyancing (buying and selling property), although as I became more competent I was also given wills to write, shares to sell, leases to draft and boundary disputes to settle. The workload was spasmodic and after just three days I was "*begging for work*". Later that same day I played for the Wragges football team against another firm. We lost the match and I lost the contents of my stomach after the opposition took advantage of the naive new boy. I felt so ill I was unable to make it in to work the next day. This was not good for my first week but thankfully there were no repercussions.

By the third week I had eight files and JHD had "*praised me for a report on title I had done for Lloyds Bank*" (basically making sure the title/ownership was correct). On days when there was little work to do I filled my time usefully getting to know people (chatting) or doing my college work, mostly the latter.

Tuesday was our day release at Matthew Boulton College. When I started, it was a bit of a "*dump*" but things improved when we later moved to brand new buildings on the Hagley Road. The four new trainees soon settled into a routine. The afternoon session on English Law was with Debley (Mr Spock). We would then have our tea at the Tow Rope cafe on Broad Street where Rod Stewart's Maggie May was constantly played on the jukebox. We returned to college for Litigation with Wilson, followed by Conveyancing with the less than impressive Wyde. None of us felt that Wyde was up to standard and after just six lectures we collectively asked him to change his teaching style with little response. There was either some improvement or we just got used to him as there were no more complaints before the end of the year.

The Birmingham Stamp Office (a government tax department) was situated a couple of streets away and I was frequently given the job of taking the documents down for stamping. This was a fairly straightforward task, or so you would think, as all I had to do was collect the deeds with their covering forms plus a cheque for the total, take them to the Stamp Office, present them to the clerk at the counter where they would be stamped and I would return to the office. Simple enough but at least three times in the first few months I forgot the cheque and had to go all the way back to the office and repeat the task.

Another regular duty, albeit a voluntary one, was "*doing the post*" for which we were paid an extra 40p per post. The number of outgoing letters from the 100 or so staff was huge. Most, if not all, of the letters were signed by the partners with some being returned each day for various reasons. At about 5pm each evening two brothers of retirement age, one called Harold the other not, would appear and begin preparing for the post. There would usually be three of us to help the brothers for about an hour or so. It took me a while to realise why my fellow trainee John Mac' was so very keen to be involved. He was attracted to, and subsequently married, another regular helper, Ann McNalty.

There were some legitimate breaks from the office. For example, before a property purchase can take place a "search" of the local authority is necessary to make sure there are no problems with matters relating to the property such as planning for development. The forms usually took a couple of weeks or longer to return. If it was an urgent transaction a personal search could take place where an individual goes to each department to complete all the enquiries. In my fourth week I carried out a personal search and due to the number of departments it took me all morning!

Property completions could take place through the post or by personal attendance. Two days after the personal search I was asked to carry out a completion in Newport, Shropshire which meant catching a train to Wellington via Wolverhampton, and taking a bus to Newport. There was the compensation of an all expenses paid (75p) three course lunch at the Barley Mow Hotel. I think I was given the trip for experience rather than it being absolutely necessary.

Just before Christmas I was instructed to catch a train to London to fetch an urgent "counsel's opinion" for one of the partners (John Hall). I was happy to oblige, as I had never been to London on the train before. The next day I was informed I was to receive a wage rise of £25. Unrelated of course.

The last day before the Christmas break was good fun with over thirty of us descending on The Cabin pub for a good old sing song and *"five Christmas kisses"* before returning to the office to take advantage of the more formal sherry party.

In those days legal firms always took an extra day off at each Bank Holiday, which meant we had five days off for Christmas including the weekend. When we did return moves were afoot: Ann Mc' (John Mac's future wife) came to sit by me as she was working for Richard Cliff, one of the solicitors who had moved into Jonathan's room after he left. I got on well with them both so this was a good way to start the New Year.

ITS FUN TO STAY AT THE YMCA.......Skegness is so bracing

I had stayed at several YMCA holiday centres with my mum and dad over the years including ones at Barry in Wales, Skegness, and their favourite, Eastbourne on the south coast. Of these Skegness had the best facilities: a large grass area suitable for cricket and football, a putting green, indoor table tennis and a snooker table making it suitable for all ages and for both families and singles alike. On a subsequent stay my friend Tez said, "All it lacks is a bar". Not many of those at the YMCA though. What it did have was regular dance evenings. The music was provided by a middle-aged couple providing old time dancing with the odd burst of "March of the Mods". The husband played the drums while his wife played the keyboard. She smiled as she swayed rhythmically to the music. It took us quite a while to realise that she was just loading a tape player! We had been duped, as had most, if not all, of the audience.

I am not sure how we decided on Skegness as a holiday destination for the boys but I would have been a strong advocate. We had been there as a family the year before my dad died and all enjoyed it immensely. Mum was still a "YMCA member" able to support our booking. Not surprisingly the other attendees were John L and Gaz.

We booked the coach at the 'Dorothy Box'. This was primarily a sweet shop at the Yew Tree in Yardley, but it also took bookings for Bowen's, the local coach firm. The Dorothy Box was run for many years by a lovely couple that got to know us lads pretty well through our regular purchases. I loved the individually wrapped chocolate nougat sold by the quarter from one of many jars stacked on the shelves, but my favourite treat was the Midland Counties ice cream's Banana Creamy Bar.

By the time it got to August we were all set for our first boys holiday. There was a slight wobble the week leading up to our departure on Saturday the 7th as I developed tonsillitis. I was sufficiently poorly to warrant calling the doctor out but fortunately I recovered enough to travel as planned. We arrived just after lunch and clarified our priorities immediately as I purchased both a hat and a football. However, our other priorities soon became clear:

Saturday 07.08.1971......"*Back at the YM saw 4 birds we fancied. Followed them to a disco, chatted them up and took them home*"

The girls were a group of friends from Bradford, West Yorkshire and seemed to have a similar outlook to us. We were of course an odd number i.e. three boys to four girls, not a bad situation to find ourselves in although it did become a bit confusing as we found out more about them. For a start two of them were called Linda and one was called Lynn. The fourth girl, Pauline was Lynn's sister. The next complication was that the sisters were expecting a visit from their boyfriends on the Sunday, although fortunately for us their car broke down on the way and they didn't make it. We saw an opportunity and took it. Later that day at the pub we paired off. I was with Lynn, Gaz with her sister Pauline, and John with one of the Linda's (Linda T as opposed to K). Which left Linda K on her own, for now.

The boyfriends turned up the next day (Monday), which meant Lynn and her sister Pauline were now off limits. We took the two Linda's out to the fairground and then to the pub (The Parrot) and I didn't waste any time:

Monday 09.08.1971 ....."*Now going out with Linda K*".

Confused? You will be! We spent the next day with the two Linda's and at night ended up at the 'Chuck Wagon' dancing until closing at 1am. The next day we bought some records that could be played in the hall where the table tennis was housed. I bought an Atomic Rooster LP (In The Hearing Of) and Gaz went for one by John Sebastian. After a disappointing visit to the Bier Keller I found myself chatting to Lynn in her room ie Pauline's sister Lynn, not to be confused with Linda K. Despite declaring that I was going out with Linda K on Monday, by Tuesday I had attracted the attention of Lynn who was very obviously keen: "*Said she was in love with me!*". This was more than a bit sudden and I was shocked by this new turn of events but didn't let that put me off '*staying a while*'!

Being a decent chap I tried to straighten things out the next morning with Linda K, as we cleared the decks for new pairings.

That night we organised a "disco" in the table tennis hall which went well considering the limited record selection. We had added T Rex's "Get It On" which was played repeatedly as you can only take so much Atomic Rooster, and dancing to John Sebastian was an even greater challenge. To our surprise the boyfriends turned up at the disco and perhaps sensing her wandering eye, Lynn's boyfriend somewhat dramatically ended their relationship during which he apparently hit her, although we did not witness any of this. Not always fun and definitely not what you would expect when you stay at the YMCA.

The decks were not quite clear as the boyfriends reappeared briefly the next morning (Friday) which led to Lynn and I taking refuge in her room until the coast was clear. Home time on the Saturday was emotional with commitments to future meetings given by both Lynn and I. What a week! Skegness WAS really very bracing.

Getting together with Lynn was all rather quick and unexpected and to have someone appear to be so keen so quickly was flattering. But although I really liked Lynn, I was clearly keeping my options open with Elaine.

Over the next four weeks letters and phone calls passed between Brum and Bradford culminating in Lynn catching the train down on my 18th birthday (17th September 1971). She came down with Linda K. Yes that is the one that I briefly accompanied in Skegness when Lynn's boyfriend arrived. I managed to persuade Gaz to look after her over the weekend. It took some doing but the boy came good.

Gaz and I met the girls at New Street station and took them to the nearest decent pub the Tavern in the Town. (This is the pub where just over three years later, twenty one people were killed by a bomb planted by the IRA). We didn't stay long and headed back to Yardley and the Ring O Bells where I consumed a strange mix of drinks:

Friday 17.09.1971...........*"Had 4 snowballs, 2 vodkas and 2 whiskies"*

Well I suppose it was a special day but what an odd combination and this was preceded by whatever I had in the Tavern and the four pints at lunchtime.;

The weekend went well. Mum bought champagne to toast my 18th. A trip into town saw some of my birthday money spent on another Atomic Rooster LP the cheerfully entitled "Death Walks Behind You" and James Taylor's "Mudslide Slim". A further visit to the Ringers and Sunday lunchtime at the Swan preceded another emotional farewell.

Coincidentally Linda T's 18th was only three weeks later. (Yes she was the one briefly paired with John L at Skegness).

Friday 08.10.1971....."*Off to Bradford to spend the weekend at Lynn's. Caught the train and arrived at 8pm. Lynn picked me up in her car (*she had just passed her driving test) *and took me to the Queens Head then home to meet her mum and dad*".

The next day I watched Lynn play really well for her hockey team as they coasted to a 5-0 victory. Linda T's party went well and Lynn and I stayed up "*chatting until 2.45am*". A quiet day on Sunday and got back to Brum at 10.30pm.

A couple of days later Lynn announced that she would probably be coming down to visit in a couple of weeks on November 4th. However, before this date arrives she dropped a BOMBSHELL:

Thursday 21.10.1971........."*Phoned Lynn at lunchtime. She said that she might join the army (this would possibly mean a move to the Birmingham area). I told her she must be mad*".

Alarm bells were ringing. This was too much too soon. Lynn was a lovely girl but this felt like far too much pressure. A couple of days later I took decisive action:

Tuesday 26.10.1971..... "*Posted a letter to end the relationship with Lynn. I thought of her throughout the day*".

The next day Lynn rang and we were finished. I was both relieved and sad but knew it was right.

RIO SENT TO COVENTRY

In mid 1970 we had started making the short trip of about 200 yards to the function room of the Yew Tree pub, called the Rio Grande suite. A progressive rock disco held every Sunday night and we thought it was great. It was officially called Sabbath Rock but we all called it "the Rio".

The regular gang of Gaz, John L, Brian, Tez and I were there most weeks. We were the locals all living within a matter of yards. Coming from further afield were the Ford brothers, Mark and Paul (the latter was known as 'Sweat" for reasons I am probably pleased to be unable to recall). There were other Central lads including Sweat's friends John Clegg, Bernie Wright, plus many more. When it came to the girls, Mark would often be there with his girlfriend Sue, plus Jean, Gaz's next door neighbour, and her friend Pam. I went twenty-four times in 1971. This would have been more often were it not for a beer strike in July forcing the Rio and many other pubs to stay shut. Added to this was the distraction of me seeing a girl throughout April and May. Her name was Jane and we met at yet another party at the home of the Ford brothers. She was in the year above me at Byng Kenrick, the Girls Grammar School next door to our school (Central G S). She lived in the same road as Mark and Paul Ford. We didn't see each other very often during our brief encounter (four weeks or so). Although in addition we did meet a few lunchtimes at the shops near the school as I have always known how to show a girl a good time! We finished at the end of May with "*nothing in common, very unemotional end*". However, I was upset to have missed several visits to the Rio.

Back at the Rio most weeks were just a great chance to "freak out", meet up with friends and have a pint or half. However, there were some interesting events. The Rio was not a massive room and we often had ten or even more in our corner. Early in the New Year our group of seven seemed to attract some unwelcome attention;

Sunday 24.01.1971..... "*Some bloke accused us of being a "team" looking for "bovver" so we left early*".

Nothing could have been further from the truth. We never saw any acts of violence, as we were a peace loving group. Not exactly flower power but certainly not looking for "*bovver*"! I did have a slightly worrying experience in the September when one of the regulars known as "*Jagger*" (due to a very slight physical resemblance to the real Mick) was rumoured to be after me with a couple of his friends. I had no idea why but was on my guard. One Sunday he made a move towards me and I was off like a shot. As I ran out of the Rio in a panic I made the mistake of turning right which was the opposite direction to where I lived. This meant that I had to keep turning right until I was back on the road leading up to the Rio. The problem was two-fold. Firstly, it was a long way, and secondly I risked running straight back into Jagger and his friends if they had gone the other way. I came back up the main road, creeping along the opposite side under the cover of darkness and made a bolt across the main road. No sign of Jagger so I was safe but knackered. Apparently, Jagger didn't make much of an effort and while I was running round the block he had returned to the comfort of the Rio.

In October we were shocked to be told that the Sabbath Rock was to leave the Rio due to poor drink sales. I had played my part in this as I rarely drank more than a pint, and often had just a half. Most of us were still at school so what do you expect! The good news was that Sabbath Rock would soon be relocating to the Sportsman's Arms on the Coventry Road. As the new venue was difficult to get to FREE transport would be provided, with coaches leaving the Rio car park every Sunday at 7pm. Net result - carry on as usual with no further to walk. Sounded good.

The first outing was on Sunday 24th October. We all went and declared the night "*a good time*". A couple of weeks later I bumped into a lad who had left my school the previous year. I was at the bar when this athletic chap spoke. "You don't remember me do you" he said somewhat pointedly. I did now, it was Frankie ("Spaza") Bates but not as I remembered him. When we had started school aged eleven Frankie wore special boots as a result of an operation to correct the alignment of his feet. Kids are cruel and he was unfortunately nicknamed Spaza Bates. He was from a family of restricted means which was evident on the week long Second Year trip to Paris. Frankie's 'luggage' consisted solely of a change of underwear and a shirt in a brown paper carrier bag while most of us had full size cases.

"No more Spaza Bates" he declared. And he was right. Much taller, fitter and well dressed. He told me he had joined the merchant navy and was now "loaded" and he could afford more than my half pint. Well done Frankie.

There were some lighter moments including a couple of "*one night stands*" (basically snogging sessions) with Jean (Gaz's neighbour) on 14th and 27th November but nothing serious. I also hooked up with Pam's sister Glynis on the 28th November, which led to me becoming a "star".

TV STAR, WELL ALMOST

Jean and her friend Pam were regulars at the Rio and now the Sportsman's Arms. Pam's younger sister Glynis had also started to make an appearance since the move to Coventry. As an attractive girl she not surprisingly had a regular boyfriend who had "Wheels" (basically a van). The only wheels we had were the ones that went round and round on the bus (or coach in our case). During our final visit of the year to the Sportsman's at the end of November Glynis and her boyfriend had a visible disagreement and split up:

Sunday 28.01.1971......."*Went to Sportsman's with Gaz, Jean, Pam. Gaz went early with Fiona and Elaine. I snogged with Glynis and took her home*".

Our "wheels" (the free coach) dropped us off at the Yew Tree (home of the old Rio). Glynis and Pam lived only a fifteen minute walk from the old Rio near to the "Ringers" pub. I often used to see Jean on the train home from work in town. The next day I asked her if she would play 'the go between" and pass on a message to Glynis via Pam (presumably they did not have a phone). Jean arranged for Glynis and I to meet up on the Friday. We had a good night out at the White Hart pub. I must have been keen because the rest of our gang went to see Elton John on the same night at the Town Hall.

A few weeks earlier I had applied successfully for two tickets to attend the recording of the popular TV show BRADEN'S WEEK (which later became "That's Life") at the BBC's Pebble Mill studios:

Saturday 04.12.1971........"*Went to see Braden's Week with Glynis. Good. Glynis was on the stage before and after. I was on tele a lot*".

When we entered the studio, everyone was directed to the left but they took one look at Glynis and led us in the opposite direction and sat us directly behind where Esther Rantzen was to sit. During the show, there was a feature about chip shops in Birmingham and Esther turned to Glynis and I and offered us a chip. Stardom! I took Glynis home and a great night ended with an arrangement to meet up the next evening near her home:

Sunday 05.12.1971........"*At night Glynis stood me up for half an hour. I went to her house. She had written me a ("Dear John") letter. So I wrote one back. I was hopping mad*".

Not surprisingly I was not happy at being dumped but being a "star" had its benefits as it was clear that I had been spotted on the box by quite a few people:

Monday 06.12.1971........"*Had a great laugh about me being a star. Walked around town with a star on. This caused the staff in Virgin records to give me 2 free plastic album covers.*"

Friday 10.12.1971........."*Went to school play. 10 people said that they saw me on Braden's week*"

Fame at last! I tried to restore things with Glynis via Jean, but to no avail. I think the boyfriend's wheels that had come off, were back on again for her! Tragically a few months later Glynis was involved in a serious car crash in which she was thrown through the windscreen. It was at this time that there was an extensive campaign to promote the use of seat belts led by Jimmy Saville under the heading "clunk click every trip". There were many posters on large billboards of people with their scarred faces and I think Glynis may have been one of them. Thankfully she made a full recovery and was as pretty as ever.

THATS ENTERTAINMENT

John's free pass (via his mum) for the ABC New Street was well used this year. I saw over thirty films and was lucky to only have to pay for two of them. All but two of the free visits were through John. The other two came via my brother Steve's work place (Lloyds Bank Priory Circus). They had connections with the nearby Gaumont cinema which enabled Steve and I to see Tora, Tora, Tora (10th March) "*very good*" and Waterloo (7th Oct) "*good*". Tora was based on the Japanese attack on Pearl Harbour and Waterloo concerned the famous battle of 1815. Probably the film I rated the best was Summer of '42 (16th July). I went with Gaz as John was on holiday with his parents in Ibiza:

Friday 16.07.1971......"*Went to the ABC New St with Gaz on John's mum's free pass. Summer of '42. Full of really funny true life features of adolescence. Had chips for tea (5p).*

Films also worth a mention are Little Big Man starring Dustin Hoffman, to whom Gaz had started to bear a resemblance (and still does); and Woodstock (18th May) that I saw with Gaz and Bri. A more challenging film was Soldier Blue (18th June) which Gaz, Brian and I paid to see at the Odeon, *"quite good, gutsy"*.

Less substantial offerings included Percy, On the Buses, Up Pompeii and a whole host of Hammer Horrors. They were all free so who could resist? Not me.

Our thirst for live music was satisfied by thirty gigs. The main venues were Birmingham Town Hall, the Odeon New Street and the Mayfair suite (sometimes called Kinetic Circus) for the bigger names. Locally we frequented the Swan (Freakies) and the Bulls Head (Hideaway) both on the Coventry Road about a twenty-minute walk from home.

The best rated nights were:

DEEP PURPLE (Town Hall) 12 Feb ....."*Good, freaked with Bri, Gaz, John, Shrimp plus John Clegg who bought my spare ticket for 12/6"*

FREE (Town Hall) 24th Feb.........."*they were brilliant. They did 3 encores. Elaine wore new maxi skirt (cord). Mark and I got the Town Hall going"*.

THE WHO (Mayfair suite) 13th May......."*They were fantastic.*

Pete Townsend was really brilliant. Gaz, Bri and Shrimp".

MOTT THE HOOPLE and PEACE (Town Hall)......."*Peace's Paul Rodger amazed me with good lead guitar work. Tight band, bluefish. Mott - incredible stage act. Rock music in the true sense. With John Clegg. Brilliant reception. The lead guitarist threw his guitar into the audience"*.

FAMILY (Town Hall) 12th November........."*Great, brilliant, really good. Went with John, Mick Shaw and Shrimp. Sat on the floor of the middle aisle"*

A slight disappointment were **LED ZEPPELIN** (Kinetic Circus) 17th Nov ...."*the vocals were much, much too loud. Jimmy Page was very good. Gaz, Mick Shaw, Shrimp and Bri taxi home".*

Not a gig, but worthy of a mention was our trip to see the musical HAIR earlier in the year with Gaz and John. .... "*Some bird* (from the cast) *asked me to dance while I was on the stage* (at the end*), Good time".* Locally the Hideway at the Bull's Head introduced a couple of enjoyable bands trying to make it to the big time including Canyon and Galliard.

There were a few near misses of bands I almost saw but got away. In October Bri and Shrimp were very lucky to get in to see **PINK FLOYD** at the Town Hall. I decided not to go which I regret a little as they were "*superb*". A week later I missed Yes as "*I was the only one that wanted to go*". My first experience of ticket touts followed four days later:

Friday 22.10.1971......."*Faces (Kinetic Circus). Tried to get tickets but they were sold out. Went up at night and tried to get in but the tout was charging too much. Bri paid £1.30 for a ticket".*

The good news is that I did get to see the Faces next year. I missed Elton John a couple of weeks later as I chose to take Glynis out. It would be over 25 years before I caught up with

Elton at Wembley stadium. The last band to get away were the Moody Blues due solely to the cost of the tickets *"we thought they were very high"*. Sadly I never caught up with them or Yes.

On the few nights that I stayed in and watched television there were still some of the old favourites such as Morecombe and Wise, Dr Finlay's casebook and Star Trek. There were also plenty of great programmes to watch such as the second series of Monty Python's Flying Circus which was now a firm favourite with the younger generation. A new American import that grabbed my attention was Alias Smith and Jones, an amusing updated western. For comedy, there was a spin off from Doctor in the House called Doctor at Large. Risqué humour was delivered by Frankie Howard and Benny Hill. For more gentle humour Nearest and Dearest could be turned to. I watched sport with BBC providing tennis from Wimbledon, test cricket and golf. As soon as the tennis started we could be found at the park with our rackets, checking to see if we had turned in to the next Bjorn Borg over the winter but the only resemblance I had was my hair style.

STILL NO JELLY AT THE PARTY

There were a dozen or more house parties held this year with the Ford residence still hosting more than its fair share. Mark and/or Paul held four. They were always good fun and usually well supported. The rest were all new venues to me including those held by Karen (27thFeb) Albert Fisher (3rd April), Maggie Chinn (29th May), Colin Bowater (3rd July), John Clegg (10th July), Elaine Jenkins (yes that one) (23rd Nov), Jill Bradley (26th Dec) and Yvonne Curtis (27th Dec).

Froggy Croton's party (17th July) was made memorable by a drunken Tez, seen snogging an even more drunk and by this time vomiting, young lady over the bath. Bri held two parties both of which were memorable in their own way. The first was at the end of July and was the only time I have ever stayed up through the night and seen the sun rise:

Saturday 31.07.1971......."*Party at Brian's. 72 people. Went off well. Tried for Yvonne but failed (*I don't remember this, especially as she was Elaine's best friend!). *Everyone enjoyed it. Finished at 12.15 am. One cushion burnt (placed on lamp to darken the room) and 2 glasses broken. John stayed until 1am to help with the clearing up (*he lived next door). *Shrimp until 2 am when Gaz came back round. Bri, Gaz, Pam, Jean and I played cards until 4am. Pam and Jean left and we talked until 5.30am when we took the empties up the road. Had sleep (6.30 to 8 am) and went to the washateria (*the local launderette)*".

Despite our efforts the house smelt like a pub for days. I'll never know how Brian managed to persuade his folks to allow him to hold a second party in December, when everyone would need to be indoors, , but he did. It was on Christmas Eve:

Friday 24.12.1971......"*Went to Giro to get booze. Bought 6 pints of lager and a bottle of lime. Went up Ringers then to Bri's party. 20 people. Finished at 12.05 am. Cleaned up until 2 am.*

Two contrasting parties. The first a great success in mid summer. The second less so but still a real achievement for Brian to hold it given the aftereffects of the first.

THE RINGERS BECOMES A SECOND HOME

There was a large gap between my first visit to the Ringers and my second as It would not be until the end of May 1971 before I revisited the Ring O Bells on Church Road Yardley. But boy oh boy when we did start to go there it soon became a regular haunt with nearly sixty visits in the last six months of the year.

In Birmingham city centre our main venue was the Parisian. This had now replaced our previous favourite the Alhambra. It was a subterranean building on two floors entered through an innocuous looking door on Cannon Street just off New Street. I recorded eleven visits including lunchtime on my 18th birthday with friends from work:

Friday 17.09.1971........."*Had 4 pints in the Parisian at lunchtime-good laugh*"

It was a popular pub that we would frequent for the next few years along with the Tavern. The Gilded Cage warranted a couple of visits, mainly for its good value lunches for which we would return in the future. After The Ringers the next most frequently visited local was The Mackadown near my old school.

But it was the Ringers that we settled into and visited most frequently. It was about a fifteen minute walk via Stoney Lane, through Gayhurst Drive and Jennifer Walk then along Church road. It had three rooms: the lounge which was named the Belfry and was too posh for us: The Bar for the hardened drinkers; definitely not us, and finally our domain, the Assembly Room. It was an Ansells pub run by Sam and Jean. They were extremely tolerant of under age drinkers who spent very little, but we were well behaved and made the pub look busy.

To start with it was just the core mainly Gaz, Tez, John and myself but we were soon joined by Jean and Pam. Steve Clayton lived at the top of our road in Heathmere Avenue and started to come along more regularly. He went to Sheldon Heath School and brought along a few friends who also became regulars, Bert (Robert Miles), Clive (Massey) and Froggy (John Croton). He was called Froggy because his voice broke before anyone else's. Some claimed he was about eleven when the notes and other things dropped. Also from Sheldon Heath was Tin (Martin Wood), who became a Ringers regular towards the end of the year.

Directly opposite the pub lived a school friend of mine, John Roden who also turned out occasionally with his near neighbours Ochband (Terrence Blackband) and Garf (Garfield Joyce). The big night at the Ringers was Friday when the numbers steadily grew over the months. Good fun was had by all although very little was drunk due mainly to our lack of funds. Another regular visitor was the seafood man with his wicker basket filled to the brim. We were encouraged to buy his goods by his tempting cry of "cockles, muscles, whelks and prawns". It didn't convince me, as I never did buy any.

A popular form of entertainment was the pub machine with its duck shoot. It was even more popular when it malfunctioned and dished out more tokens than it should. I was not a gambler and rarely played the machine so did not benefit. I wasn't much of a drinker either with half of lager and lime my usual at this time. Gaz was a brown and mild man, and John drank straight bitter, as did Tez. During the year I made over one hundred visits to more than twenty different pubs but drank less than two hundred pints. No wonder Ansells brewery closed before long.

SUNDAYS AFTER THE ARCHERS

Most Sundays started with the radio playing next to my bed. I would start by listening to Alistair Cooke's Letter from America that ran for an amazing fifty-seven years. This was a fifteen-minute insight into what was interesting him on the other side of the pond. Then came my weekly fix of the Archers. Sadly, I lost touch with Ambridge a long time ago.

My brother Steve and I were still fairly regular attendees at the "Gospel Hall" (aka the Hall) on Waterloo Road, as we had been for as long as we could remember. Friends would ask why I still went most Sunday mornings. I had a couple of reasons: it was to some degree a well grooved habit, I liked most of the people there, but the overwhelming reason was that it made me feel like I was part of a large welcoming family as my own was shrinking to just my Mum, brother and Granddad. Whether my Dad's sudden death played a part in my continued attendance I am not too sure. I never committed to the religious side but there was never any pressure to take 'the dip', a full immersion was practised for baptism regardless of age. However, I am sure the experience had a positive effect on my moral compass.

Steve and I had grown up with the other young people including Richard and Joy Beresford (next door neighbours), Ann and Jane Yardley (Beresford's cousins), Dilys and Lynn (friends of the Yardley girls). There were also a couple of other attractive girls, June and Evelyn. In our teens the informal hour evolved into discussions about a wide range of subjects from drug use, the history and development of swear words, to the role of ambition. I enjoyed my other family and it was really this that kept me going. We even had holidays together including visits to Wales and the Isle of Wight.

NEW YEARS EVE

As usual the last evening of the year was spent with friends and family at the home of the Yardleys' in Vicarage road. My diary records *"about 35 people there. Dilys looked great. Home at 3.45am"*.

CHAPTER 3 1972: Riviera highlight

In the big wide world, there was plenty going on in 1972. There were signs that the Vietnam War was cooling as the USA ended the draft and peace talks began in Paris. SALT 1 (Strategic Arms Limitation Talks) was signed in May, a first step in trying to control nuclear weapons. The space race between the USA and USSR continued with a Soviet landing of an unmanned vessel on the moon and the Americans making two manned landings with Apollo 16 and 17. Meanwhile American president Richard Nixon was heading for future problems as a national scandal began with a break in at The Watergate Hotel. Tragedy struck at the Munich Olympics when terrorists killed eleven people.

On a lighter note a Japanese soldier was found in the Guam jungle, some twenty six years after the war had ended. Home entertainment was revolutionised by "PONG" the first video game launched by Atari.

Back in the UK strikes were prevalent in the dockyards, mines and car factories. Power cuts disrupted normal life for many. Unemployment rose to over a million for the first time since the Second World War. There was unrest in Ireland with Bloody Sunday occurring and the IRA bombed the mainland at Aldershot.

But all of that was far away from everyday life in Yardley Birmingham.

THEY THINK IT'S ALL OVER

To quote the late football commentator Kenneth Wolstenholme "It is now!". The final parting with Elaine was so unplanned that neither of us realised it had happened at the time. Consequently, there were no goodbyes, no tears or gnashing of teeth. With hindsight, it was probably the best way to end, even though our last date was on her birthday (25th February).

In the weeks leading up to this we had seen a fair amount of each other beginning with a memorable event at the Sportsman's Arms (resited Rio) on the 2nd January when Gaz celebrated his seventeenth birthday by throwing up on the coach on the way home. I described the evening with Elaine as a "*one night stand*", but we were soon out together again enjoying concerts by Free, Procol Harum and Mountain. Added to this was a trip to the cinema with Gaz and Fiona plus a couple of visits to her house. We exchanged Valentine's cards, "*a large (enormous) card from Elaine*" but in hindsight I think this had been posted prior to us meeting up and before we realised that all was not well:

Friday 11.02.1972...."*went to Elaine's with Gaz and Fiona. I treated Elaine very badly. Home at 12.30 am*".

I don't know what I did but I am sure it didn't help and probably made Elaine regret sending such an 'enormous' card. We saw each other at the Strawbs concert a couple of days later. I then rang to invite her out on her birthday;

Friday 25.02.1972.... "*Elaine's birthday. Went with Elaine, Gaz and Fiona plus Bri, Shrimp and John L to the Mackadown. Elaine drunk. Stayed until 11.45. Home 12.10am*".

This was most unlike her. In fact I don't ever remember seeing her like that before. There was no meaningful contact between us after that as we started to drift apart, but it could have been very different.

Just ten days later Elaine's dad rang me at work asking me to act in their sale and purchase as they were on the move. It turned out that they had looked at the house next door but one to us in Charminster Avenue. In the end they settled for a house on Church Road, the same road as the "Ringers" but the other side of the church. It would have been interesting if instead they had bought the one so very close to me.

I completed the sale and purchase and they moved in on the 26th May. Within a few days Elaine held a party in their new home to which we were all invited. The party on June 3rd underwhelmed me! Was it sour grapes as Elaine was now seeing Trevor Clarke He also went to Saltley and was the brother of Elaine's school friend, Sue. Elaine now lived so close to the "Ringers" we were bound to bump into each other and very soon we did. We nicknamed Trevor "the dog" as he seemed to be on a short lead. Probably very unfair as they did go on to marry, possibly too young though because they sadly divorced later.

BERNIE THE BOLT

Bernie Wright was in the year above me at Central. Our paths crossed due mainly to our mutual friendship with his school pals Paul (Sweat) Ford and John Clegg (JC). We played together in the school cricket team occasionally and were both at many parties held at Mark and Paul Ford's house. We also shared the same birthday, albeit a year apart.

He was an outstandingly powerful athlete and performed to a high standard in almost every sport. He excelled at rugby and athletics with soccer probably his weakest discipline. He was, however, on the books of Birmingham City before moving to Walsall in 1971. In February 1972 Walsall drew Everton away in the FA cup where Bernie impressed the Everton management so much they signed him on the 9th February for £40,000. At nineteen this was a fabulous opportunity. Five weeks after his move I had occasion to look him up:

Tuesday 14.03.1972 … *"Train to Liverpool. Took files for Ivor Edwards (partner) Went to Everton training ground by taxi to see Bernie. Watched them train then had lunch (in canteen).*

Sat with Howard Kendall and Henry Newton. Went for drink. Home (New St) at 5.14pm"

I was treated so well by everyone at the club and was impressed by their fantastic facilities. Bernie's time at Everton was to be less than a year but I did get to watch him play for Everton reserves at Villa Park in October. He was very friendly with his old school friend John Clegg who had started work at Wragges in the summer also as a trainee Legal Executive. We met Bernie for a drink in the Parisian the Monday following the reserve game. He played only eleven first team games for Everton scoring two goals. He fell from grace after laying out the coach, Stuart Imlach, when he failed to be selected for the team. Stuart mentions this incident in his autobiography. Soon afterwards Bernie was back at Walsall.

SKEGGY FAR LESS BRACING (1st to 8th June)

This turned out to be a very different holiday compared to our visit the previous year. There were now four of us, John L, my brother Steve and Tez who replaced Gaz.

It didn't start well as I left my jumper on the coach. Luckily I got it back. The big disappointment was the lack of any groups of girls (*"no birds at YMCA"*). There was, however, plenty of sport to enjoy: cricket (*"scored over 50"*), football, putting, table tennis and snooker. We even joined in the sports day where John and I won the three-legged race and I came second in the sack race.

At other times, we visited the fair, played bingo and even caught a bus to the pitch and putt course. The evenings were spent in the local pubs. We revisited one of the previous year's haunts, The Parrot, and discovered that, sadly, *the* parrot had died during the winter, it was no more, it had ceased to be. Fortunately, the pub itself hadn't died. We went there a couple of times during our stay but preferred the livelier Variety Bar which had comedians and groups to entertain us until late.

We did have fun with some other lads including a victorious pillow fight. Despite having a good time, it did not live up to the previous year, or our expectations.

A TOUCH OF THE ENGLISH RIVIERA

Just four weeks after returning from a less than exciting week at the YMCA Holiday Centre in Skegness, six of us were off to try a different YMCA Holiday Centre at Torquay on the English Riviera. The decision was made back in January and Gaz, Tez and I were joined by first timers Bri, Shrimp and Steve C.

The coach set off on the evening of Friday 12th August at 11.15pm. A long drive through the night saw us arrive at Torquay's coach park at the ungodly hour of 5.20am. Fortunately it was a glorious morning. We found the YMCA and declared the view from its cliff top location as *"fantastic"*. We dropped off our luggage and found a cafe for breakfast, which opened at 7am. The next place to open was the betting shop. I placed a 30p bet, which later that day turned into £1.87. This was gambling on the Riviera with style! After breakfast and betting we settled down by the harbour and waited for the rest of Torquay to stir.

It was such a beautiful day that, after lunch at the Castle pub, we went down to the beach and swam in the sea. At night, we went back to the Castle pub and then took a look around the town and it's many other pubs.

This was a very different YMCA, much more like a hotel but with fewer facilities. It benefitted from its great location, which was made to look even better by the superb weather. On the Sunday morning we made use of the table tennis and snooker tables. Then in the afternoon we discovered there we at least two groups of girls staying there! Gaz focused on one group whilst I got chatting to a couple of girls who were there with their family. This turned out to be in my favour;

Sunday 13.08.1972......*"after lunch Gaz chatted to some birds which led me to get off with Christine (German bird)"*.

She was born here but her Mum and Dad were German. He was the Pastor of a Lutheran church in Cambridge and she was visiting Torquay with her younger sisters.

The next morning Christine and I took a boat trip across the bay to the small fishing port of Brixham. I was not particularly impressed but the weather was *"bostin"* (Brummie speak, translation, "great"). The afternoon saw a visit to the beach and an 'event' that is still recalled by the core gang to this day. Chris declared that she did not have the appropriate attire for swimming. She decided to wear a white T-shirt and shorts. The hot weather and cool sea were too much to resist and Chris soon joined us in the waves. It was immediately apparent that her impromptu clothing was not as appropriate as she had envisaged, as when she left the sea and walked calmly along the beach, heads turned, as one, in her direction. WOW!

That night Chris and I went to the pictures to see the French Connection and returned by taxi. Not my usual mode of transport, I was obviously out to impress. The hot and sunny weather continued but the gang still managed to spend some time indoors playing table tennis, snooker and listening to Gaz's "Who's Next " album. The following evening, I took Chris for a drink and we stayed up talking until 2.15am. We spent a lot of time just walking and talking as we got to know each other. The following day the gang had an important decision to make as the rock group "Hawkwind" were playing at the Town Hall on the Wednesday evening. I was never into them and I had a much better alternative. I think just Bri and Steve C went in the end. Instead Chris and I went to the Yacht pub (now the Cinnabar), then went for a long stroll through the gardens of the Hommers Hotel (now apartments). It is rumoured that Gary Glitter and Denise Van Outen stayed there as a couple in the early 90's when she was just seventeen, a similar age to Chris. We returned to the Yacht pub the next day where many drinks were consumed by the others, particularly Bri *"who got drunk and went in the sea with his clothes on"*. It might be said that he was "doing a Chris"!

Before our goodbyes, we spent as much time as we could together and a surprisingly close relationship developed on both sides. Was this just another holiday romance? An early start home followed:

Saturday 19.08.1972....*"a long and lonely coach journey, but it was NOT TOO BAD with the lads having a laugh. At night we all went to the Ringers and talked".*

I phoned Chris the next day and we agreed to meet up as soon as possible. This seemed to be happening quickly as, after a few more phone calls, a visit to Cambridge was arranged for the following Sunday (Bank Holiday weekend). The plan was then changed to Chris coming to Brum only for her Dad to intervene *"for our benefit"*. Tears were shed and it seemed to be all over.

However, a surprise phone call late the next evening gave me hope. At 11.30pm, after I returned from seeing Hitchcock's Frenzy with John L and Steve C, Chris's sister Anne rang to try and help. The result was a return to phone calls and the possible resurrection of a visit to Cambridge.

Very quickly a trip was set for just one week later, on Friday 1st September. I borrowed a sleeping bag and Froggy Croton lent me his Youth Hostel card. Two days were booked off work and train tickets purchased. I was all set. I arrived at 7pm on the Friday and took my kit to the Youth Hostel. Chris and I went to the pub and then back to her home to borrow a bike to return to the hostel.

The next morning after completing my mandatory chores at the hostel, I met up with Chris and spent a pleasant day around the town including strolling along the "backs" of the river Cam. There was one slight problem:

Saturday 02.09.1972....*"At Chris's I broke a window playing football (on my own) in huge garden of a huge house".*

It was huge because primarily it was a church although not the traditional C of E model. It was in a residential street but the building contained a large meeting room plus accommodation for the Pastor and his family. It turned out that Chris's parents were away and she was looking after her sisters. The hostel closed at 10.30pm and *"I had to run like the clappers"* to avoid being locked out. The hostel rules limited my stay to three nights and on the last morning the police arrived and we all had our kit searched for a missing camera, which was not recovered. Chris's parents returned and I am not sure they were expecting me to be there but they were most hospitable. We even played a tennis doubles match that Chris and I lost. For my last night, I was kindly invited to kip down in the meeting area, which was a bit spooky, even though I had company for a while.

The last day was spent walking, talking and saying our goodbyes. Sadly, it was the day the Israeli team suffered a fatal attack by the Black September group at the Munich Olympics. It must have been even more of a shock for Chris's German born parents.

Having got back to Brum the phone line was hot and letters exchanged. More remarkable still was that I wrote my one and only poem. This was serious! Her Dad, however, did his best to put a stop to us. I didn't really know why, and his efforts didn't work very well as we were still having numerous long phone calls.

By the middle of October, the calls from Cambridge had become less frequent and I suspected that her Dad's influence, albeit well meant, was winning. I tried to ring and was told on more than one occasion that Chris was out. On Friday the thirteenth the "Dear John" letter arrived:

Friday 13.10.1972…"*had letter. Chris and I are now finished. Her old man, and now she has a fella. Don't mind anyway. Put £10 in the Halifax.*"

I did mind, of course, I really did, but it was not a surprise. I suspected the "fella" may have been a student who had gone home for the summer and had now returned, but this could have just been a way of me dealing with the break up. I think her dad was looking after me as well as Chris. That night I went out and (very unlike me), I tried to drown my sorrows with five pints of lager at the Wayfarer, Hockley Heath. It didn't work!

Despite my very strong feelings I was never one to let the grass grow under my feet. I kept my options open by asking Dilys (Hawker) out to see The Godfather on John's free pass. She was an intelligent, attractive girl with a certain mystique, but unfortunately, after Chris, the essential spark was missing and this was our only date. The film was good though, even on a second viewing.

WORK GROWS BUT NOT WITHOUT SOME FRUSTRATION

Starting work at Wragge & Co the previous September had taken some adjusting to. The official hours were nine to five but if you arrived on time you would find only a few people there. The bus trip from the Yew Tree to town took about 20 to 25 minutes depending on the traffic and my usual arrival time was about 9.15am. My diary regularly notes my intention to get up earlier, which is surprising given the general apathy towards punctuality.

After Steve C left school in the summer and started work for accountants Farmiloe & Co, he would often call for me and we would travel together into town. After he passed his driving test he was often able to borrow his Mum's car and take us in, timing our arrival for after 9am, as his firm was just as lax as mine. Given the relaxed attitude I found it particularly challenging to wake in time for work when Mum was away on holiday with my Grandad or her friend Hilda. One morning when my brother Steve was also working away, I managed to sleep through two alarm clocks, my next-door neighbour's knock on the door, Steve C's knock and finally my Grandad's pre-arranged wake up phone call. I can't remember what time I arrived into work that morning.

I found the often slow pace of work frustrating and regularly asked for more files. I also quickly realised the "them and us" situation. Although I was training to be a Legal Executive I could never be a partner and share in the spoils and joys of running the business. You had to be a qualified lawyer to be one of them! Four of us had been taken on as trainees Michael (Mick) O'Mahoney, John McCormack (John Mac) and John Hunter (aka the scout). Before the year was out, Scout had decided to go to law school and qualify via the long route, the others also later followed this path. Eventually I was the only one of us that didn't take the long hard route to becoming a qualified solicitor. I couldn't face the huge amount of work, years of study and initially limited income. My mood fluctuated mainly with the workload, or lack of it as well as with receiving comments on my appearance:

Thursday 06.01.1972...."*JHD (my managing partner) had me in to review my files. He also told me in a very nice sort of way that I should have my hair trimmed*".

This was 1972 and the fashion was for us chaps to have longer hair. I didn't have the trim, but a few weeks later Mr Morgan the Practice Manager (not qualified) had a word:

Thursday 24.02.1972, "*Morgan had me in his office re hair. Went alright but insulted*".

I can see now why I was "*treated like a 2-year-old*" on occasions, as time was needed to build up knowledge and confident handling of the workload, but I was impatient. There were lots of lighter moments, though. The two partners' secretaries, Ann and Jane, who sat opposite me were great fun, helpful and very supportive. They were both a bit older than me with Jane married and Ann single but with a steady boyfriend. They pulled my leg a lot but also did a lot of my typing and covered for me on occasions.

One of my duties was to look after the library, which was just around the corner from my desk. On the face of it this may have seemed a menial task but it had some distinct advantages. Firstly, I could make sure I had the books I needed. Not surprisingly one of the most popular books came from the twenty or so volumes of the Encyclopedia of Forms and Precedents. The law, particularly property law, has numerous forms to suit many situations. From memory, volumes eleven and twelve contained those most frequently used and were often in demand. I rarely had a problem procuring these and became a useful contact for some of the conveyancers. Once a week, usually a Friday afternoon, I would make a tour of the whole office to collect unwanted books. This had the dual benefits of chatting and getting to know a lot of the staff and also rescuing the books in demand. What I didn't appreciate at the time was how useful this duty would prove in a future job application.

There were seventeen partners plus a consultant, G. Corbyn-Barrow. He was one of the Cadbury family and a former Lord Mayor of Birmingham. We thought he was about a hundred or at least eighty but I now realise he was only sixty-eight when I joined; he went on to reach the ripe old age of ninety four. All the senior partners seemed old to us 'youngsters'. I thought that Charles Chatwin was about seventy but I now know that he had a relatively famous son, Bruce Chatwin a successful author of both travel books and novels. This puts his dad Charles around his mid-fifties at the time. One person who was truly old, however, was Jim Gannaway, one of the old managing clerks. He was a legend at Wragges and had been there forever. He wrote everything out by hand, was always pleasant to everyone and came and went as he pleased. Apart from his work, his second passion was Walmley Sports Club, of which he was an honorary life member. He could take a joke too, as we referred to him in the office cabaret as "running the clapped out clerks". Dear Jim.

We had two solicitors with sight problems. Mr Jarvis, was completely blind; and one of the partners, Mr Lowsley, was partially sighted. The latter used a mini telescope attached to his glasses to help him read. As I am partially sighted I can identify with them both, particularly Mr Lowsley. It was very non-pc but it amused us to refer to them as "BLINK and HALF BLINK".

Blink had a full time "reader" who did just that. He sat with Blink and read his papers out to him. He also accompanied him when necessary. The thing that amused us was that the reader dressed more like a lawyer than anyone else in the building, even down to a bowler hat. He was immediately christened "Odd Job" after the character in Goldfinger.

Mr Jarvis was fiercely independent and travelled alone to work each day by train. I am not sure if he had a white cane but he had to negotiate his way from New Street Station to Windsor House, crossing a couple of busy roads. This he managed successfully, but one day news spread around the office that something had happened. It was reported that when his train arrived in the station he opened the carriage door and exited as usual. Unfortunately, not all of the train had fully entered the station and he stepped out and landed on the track. Fortunately, he was not badly hurt and he was soon back to normal. How much of this was exaggerated by the time it reached me I do not know.

There were three married couples, at the firm, John (Solicitor) and Sally Darby (Partner's Secretary); Fred (middle aged Legal Executive known as "Fred on Title" after the conveyancing bible "Emmet on Title") and Mrs Preece; and finally Bert and Mrs M Norway. There were also several office romances such as John Mac' and Ann McN', John Crabtree and Carol and probably many more that we didn't get to know about. My own involvement with the young ladies of the firm had so far been limited to a few very innocent kisses in the Cabin pub at Christmas, but this was about to come back to me with a bang.

When I started at Wragges we had a couple of office juniors, Jeff and Sue. They did deliveries around town, helped with the post at night and any other tasks set by the office manager, Mr Dolphin. Jeff was about 17 and a very helpful and pleasant lad who had aspirations to eventually move into a clerical position. Sue was a quiet girl of a similar age to Jeff, but with much better legs that she was keen to show off with her very short skirts. She was not unattractive but perhaps a little "unsophisticated" and she left soon after Christmas.

One morning in March, Jeff rushed up to my desk in a slight panic to inform me that Sue's "biker" boyfriend was out by the lifts and wanted to see me. Jeff said the biker was in a foul mood and warned me to be careful. Feeling on edge I immediately went down to the floor below to summon the help of John Mac' who was well over 6 feet tall and looked as though he could handle himself. Good mate John came upstairs and we went out into the corridor. Before I had chance to exchange pleasantries with the "biker", I received a blow to my face. John grabbed the biker and threw him into a lift telling him not to return. He was still mouthing off about what I had done to his girlfriend as the lift doors closed. I was in shock and distinctly puzzled about what she had told him. All that for a Christmas kiss! It was a little bit out of kilter to say the least. John said he thought that would be the end of it but I still went out through the delivery area in the basement for the next few days. Fortunately, biker boy heeded John's warning and didn't return.

There was more excitement of a different kind a few days later when a request came from the police for some volunteer lads of our age to take part in an identity parade. Even better we were to be paid 50p for our trouble. This was more than we got for an hour on the post.

Thursday 23.03.1972....*" In the afternoon I went to an identity parade at Steelhouse Lane police station. I was nearly chosen as the criminal"*.

I looked nothing like him, as he was taller than me and with ginger hair. The witness eventually selected the right one after having more than one look at yours truly.

Despite these interludes, I was not happy and started to seriously consider another career. I had talked to one of the lads at day release (Paul Taylor) whose girlfriend was training to be a teacher at St Peters College Saltley. I discussed this with my Mum and brother Steve and decided to apply to become a P.E. teacher. Given my modest academic record I sought the help and support of my favourite teacher, Brian Hutton who lived close by and whose lodgings we passed regularly on the way to the "Ringers". He was most encouraging and offered to provide a reference, even suggesting applying to Loughborough College where he had some contacts. I decided to stick to St Peters and made an application. An interview soon followed:

Tuesday 22.02.1972...."*Interview at St Peters. Had two interviews one with the head of PE. Nice chap,got on great. Had a test. 50/50 chance of getting in"*.

I was being optimistic as usual and a couple of days later I received the rejection letter. It appeared to be my lack of 'A' levels that let me down and they suggested I take 'A' level law and reapply. I didn't. Instead I studied hard for my legal exams and was delighted to pass them both. Wragges were very supportive and gave us time off to study, which I took full advantage of. All four of us passed both parts, with the Scout gaining distinctions in both subjects. He left shortly after to pursue the real thing and we all wished him well with a £2.50 book token.

There was good news in July when a friend from my school, John Clegg joined the firm. JC was in the year above at Central but we had already become friends via the Ford brothers and going to the same parties and concerts. He lived nearby and had started to come to the Ringers. This made a difference and the three of us (including Mick O'Mahoney) gelled and I began to settle.

My workload gradually grew and by the time college restarted in September I had 59 files. The college had moved to a smart new tower block on the Hagley Road, the downside being no Tow Rope Cafe although the college had a canteen and a football table. A pay rise in October taking my salary to £800 also helped to encourage my endeavours. Each month the partners were circulated with an update of the fee earnings. These were confidential but I managed to sneak a look that October, which revealed mine to be £1300 for the first nine months of the year. I was therefore on target to hit c£1600 for the full year, which would be about twice my salary. There were considerable support costs to be paid before the partners would see any personal benefit, but it occurred to me that this was a reasonable start from scratch.

Wragges occupied floors six and seven of Windsor House which was next door to the Rackhams department store. Not to be confused with the local saying and connotation "back of Rackhams!" Things were getting pretty cramped. In October, it was announced that we had agreed to occupy part of the eighth floor and that I would be moving up there with JHD (partner), Bob Gilbert (solicitor), Paul Howard (Articled Clerk) plus Ann (JHD's Secretary). We moved in on the 1st November and I was happy despite losing my favourite desk, which I had secured when Mr Lowsley (Half Blink) had a new one. The decor was different from floor seven as we had carpet tiles as opposed to vinyl, and the walls were newly painted orange and brown. These were Ann Taylor's choice and were very seventies! The other good news was that we had a table tennis table in a spare room, which we used frequently. I wasn't too bad but Mike Wooldridge (Articled Clerk) was the champion.

Mike was from Worcester and had the county twang to match, which led to him being called "muck spreader". Not surprisingly he did not appreciate this. His retaliation was to call me Eamon after the footballer Eamon Dunphy who was currently playing for Millwall. The link between Duffin and Dunphy was fairly tenuous but it stuck, well it did for Mike. He was a talented leg spin bowler and played cricket for the Worcester County second team. One of the surprising things about the training set up, or rather the lack of it, was that we trainee legal execs, had the new intake of articled clerks with their law degrees and Part 1's asking us for help on their files. Although this did not last long as they soon made up ground, this was taking "sitting with Nellie" a bit too far. Mike was no exception and at times in the early days drove me mad, but later we became good friends. One of these poor chaps, Paul Howard, who was in our small enclave on the eighth floor, broke his leg playing rugby. I benefitted from his misfortune by minding his files while he recovered. As the year closed I was feeling more appreciated and learning fast. Writing and rehearsing for the annual office cabaret began. Surprisingly the partners were disappointed if they were not the target of our boyish humour.

IT'S FRIDAY, IT'S NINE O'CLOCK, IT'S THE RINGERS

Friday was the night that saw the biggest turn out of the lads in the Assembly Room of the Ring O'Bells. Our record was twenty eight on the 4th February. This number included friends of friends but was still an impressive turn out. It was not just Fridays that were spent in the Ringers, I recorded my total visits for the year to our local as a staggering 139, almost 40% of available days. Despite this the total number of pints consumed averaged just over one per day at 401 for the whole year (in all of the pubs, not just the Ringers). Although I didn't drink much it was a great place to meet, chat and just have fun. We sometimes laughed until we cried and also teased people until they "cracked up".

There were a couple of incidents that took place just outside the pub. Tez had an ongoing problem with a couple of lads from his old school that had led to him being attacked and badly bruised in the car park on Good Friday at the end of March. Unfortunately, as it was a Bank Holiday there were hardly any of our usual crowd there and I felt a little guilty for not being around. We all got a telling off from his Dad for not intervening but I didn't have the heart to say I wasn't there.

Apart from the core gang, the Ringers' regulars began to include a couple more of Steve Clayton's school friends, namely Luigi (Alvaro Damiani) and Peg (David Yates). From Central GS there was John Clegg, Pete Olive, John Roden, and John Hargreaves. Finally, there was Garf (Garfield Joyce) who went to Saltley but was friends with most of us either from junior school (my year at Hobmoor) or because he lived close to the Ringers in Homecroft and then there was his mate, Keith Gadsby. There were others on the edge of the group plus, of course, a small number of girls who drifted in and out and about whom we will hear more later.

Ochband lived less than 100 yards from the Ringers and we would often either begin or end the evening at his house playing cards for small amounts. He also introduced us to collecting beermats, which then led to the competitive skill of flipping a whole pile and catching the return without dropping any. By the end of the year I had peaked at forty two mats flipped on 27th December. "Flipping Heck"!

Other distractions from the Ringers included a phase of visiting the Silver Blades ice rink in town. We seemed to enjoy several trips there in February but the attraction soon wore off as we reached a certain level of incompetence, and we returned to the Ringers to do what we did best. We resumed our usual dive into tennis as soon as Wimbledon started although the racquets went back in the garage soon after Stan Smith and Billie Jean king had triumphed.

WHEELS ROLL UP

Our visits to the Ringers peaked in the month of June at twenty one. Yes, it was the summer with long light nights but the main reason for the visits dropping to around 10 per month was the introduction of CARS! By this time several of the lads had passed their driving tests: Bert, Pete O, Peg and Keith G even had their own wheels. A mixture of Ford Anglia's and Austin A40's but they all had "go faster" sports steering wheels. Steve C had passed his test and had access to his Mum's car so we were on the grid itching to leave the Ringers behind and boldly go where none of us had gone before.

Not surprisingly we started off visiting good pubs that were not too far away such as the Red House, Saracens Head and the Wayfarer, all of which were in the Solihull area. We moved on to the Bear at Berkswell and the Bull at Barston, as we became more upwardly mobile. There would be as many as a dozen or more of us in different combinations of the five cars. Bert used to drive his car flat out at times, whereas Pete would try to look cool with his driving gloves and sports steering wheel. Fortunately, there were no crashes and no excessive drinking behind the wheel although there were a couple of incidents involving the police. On the 9th September Steve C was caught speeding doing 55mph in a 30 limit. This was embarrassing for the son of a police sergeant driving a very old Austin A35 (they stopped making them in 1959). Exactly a week later thirteen of us were out celebrating my nineteenth birthday and were stopped by the police at Birmingham Airport on our way back from the Saxon Mill but we were just told to carry on. We gradually moved further afield to Kenilworth and Stratford on Avon but the Ringers was still our local, especially during the week. I soon caught the driving bug and started lessons:

Wednesday 01.11.1972… *"Had my first driving lesson today. Did quite well. Went up the Coventry Road to the Wheatsheaf pub and around"*

The instructor had a strong Irish accent and ran the Oxford School of Motoring, so called after the road in which he lived in Acocks Green. His favourite saying was "now for a little bit of braking". Very appropriate on my first lesson which was in the dark and before I knew I needed glasses for driving. After just four lessons (plus the two I had from my brother the previous year) he gave me a form to complete for my test. Now who is being over optimistic?

I have never really been interested in the actual cars so it was surprising that in October I booked a day off work to go to the Motor Show. Steve C, Keith G and I set off for Earls Court, London, at 8.25am in Steve's Mum's car and spent three hours at the show. The highlight was the John Player Special racing car, which drew lots of interest, as did the scantily clad young ladies helping to promote their product. We arrived home just after midnight and I described the day out as *"very good"* with the total cost at £3.

There were a couple of the lads who stayed on two wheels for a while. Clive Massey's Dad ran a motorbike shop which obviously influenced Clive's decision. The other was Martin (Tin) Wood who rode a Yamaha125 and managed to stay on… most of the time. He can still be found on two wheels but now relies on pedal power.

BLOOMERS BLOSSOMS

Looking for a change of scene from the Sportsman's Arms (resited Rio) we tried something new in May. There was a night club opposite the Swan in the Tivoli Shopping Centre called the Cavendish Club about 15 minutes' walk from home. It had recently been relaunched as "Bloomers" featuring mainly pop bands and disco rather than the previous dinner/cabaret style entertainment. We often went on a Sunday and although the music was far more mainstream than we were used to, we visited about ten times before the year was out.

The main attendees were the usual suspects i.e. Gaz, Tez, John L and Bri, although Tin, Steve C, Pete O, Keith G and Garf sometimes joined us. The bouncers were quite strict on age and attire. Both Gaz and Bri were refused admission at different times, which put us off for a little while. With Tez towering over everyone including the bouncers, he was frequently offered a job "on the door" but quite sensibly declined.

BANDS

In comparison to 1971 we saw fewer bands focusing on the bigger names and larger venues in the centre of town. On the list were:

Procol Harum (Town Hall) 19.01.1972...... *"very good, enjoyed them very much, did Salty Dog etc. Amazing Blondel, fair, With Elaine, Yvonne, Fiona, Gaz, John L, John Clegg and Shrimp".*

Wishbone Ash 28.01.1972... *"with John Clegg. Really brilliant. Great guitar work with two leads. Town Hall full. 4 encores. Great time. Sweat and Jill also there".*

Free (Town Hall) 02.02.1972...*'Really brilliant, excellent. Paul Rogers was cavorting more than ever. 2 encores, the second with the lights on. Elaine, Yvonne, Fiona, Gaz and John L. John Mac and Anne there. I am taking Elaine out".*

Mountain (Mayfair Suite) 07.02.1972... *"with Elaine, Yvonne, Gaz, Bri and Shrimp. Fair. Had a lift home from Yvonne's Dad"*.

Strawbs (Town Hall) 15.02.1972...."*very good, didn't like a couple of songs (Sheep and Tomorrow) but rest very good. With Elaine, Yvonne, Fiona, Gaz and Bri'*.

Osibisa 16.03.1972... *"at Mayfair suite with Bri. Great, excellent. Home 12.39am"*.

David Bowie 17.03.1972....."*left work early. Went to Town Hall with Bri and Gaz (not full). David Bowie-fair, Mr Crisp - fair"*.

Mungo Jerry 28.07.1972..."*went to see Mungo Jerry at Top Rank with Pete Olive and others. Fair"*. (Pete O a big MJ fan!)

Faces 22.10.1972 (Mayfair suite)..."*went to see the Faces with Pete O, Steve C, John L and John C. Very good. Packed and hot"*.

Emerson Lake and Palmer 24.11.1972.. *"Mob went to see ELP at the Odeon (New Street). Very good. Went in the Windsor first"*.

Barclay James Harvest 27.11.1972 ...*"left work at 5.05 pm because Bri, Steve C (his car), and Keith went to see Barclay James Harvest at the Civic Hall Wolverhampton plus Camel. Very good. Home at 12pm"*.

Family 06.12.1972... *"John C, Pete O, Bri, John L, Keith and I went to see Family at the Town Hall. Very good"*.

I was now earning so you would expect my album purchases to increase, but I only bought half a dozen or so including a second hand copy of Fire and Water (by Free), and new albums Catch Bull at Four (Cat Stevens), Santana's Abraxas and a very unimpressive 3 Friends from Gentle Giant.

FREE PASS PLEASURE

I only went to see a dozen or so films this year but the quality of film choice had obviously improved from the previous year. Best film was "The Godfather" which I saw twice, with John L and also with Dilys. I rated it as *"really good"* the first time and *"very good"* the second time. Runners up were Hitchcock's "Frenzy" and the classic war film "Where Eagles Dare", all receiving *"very good"* ratings. A disappointing *"alright"* was awarded to "Straw Dogs" despite the appearance of Susan George; and The French Connection only warranted a *"quite good"*. Picking up a rotten tomato was Ken Russell's "The Devils" which is the only film I have ever walked out on. I described it as *"Perverted Rubbish"*! No punches pulled there. Morecambe and Wise in the 'Intelligence Men' and the TV spin off 'Please Sir' provided lighter moments. Going to see "Mary Queen of Scots" with Jean was a mistake in more ways than one.

On the small screen I was really into Monty Python and would always try to make sure I was home to catch it as there were no video recorders back then. Similar in comedy style but more mainstream were the Goodies whose roots were in radio's "I'm Sorry I'll Read That Again". I found the "Doctors" comedy series, "Doctor at Large" on my comedy wave length, but could also enjoy the more family orientated Morecambe and Wise as well as the impressionist Mike Yarwood.

There were new programmes coming out all the time., I particularly liked the drama, 'The Brothers' following it for the next few years. This was about a family haulage business with lots of twists and turns, and several on and off relationships. Although the war had been over for many years I found the "Colditz" series one not to miss. The department store comedy "Are You Being Served" also started its long run with Mrs Slocombe's pussy becoming the talk of the Ringers. One series that started in the September of 1972, and is still running today, was "Mastermind" -it started but it hasn't finished!

FOOTBALL CRAZY

Not working on a Saturday anymore meant that I could go to watch Villa play more regularly. I usually went with John L and his Dad although occasionally I would be offered a seat by our near neighbours; the Eccles, with whom my Dad used to sit for many years in the Witton Lane stand (rebuilt for the 1966 World Cup). Joe Eccles had played a few times for the Villa many years previously. They always provided coffee at half time and I soon recognized the distinctive addition of brandy! The end of the 1971/72 season in May saw the boys promoted and return to the old second division with a record number of points (seventy). This was impressive back when only two points were awarded for a win! I only went to one away game that season but it turned out to be quite an experience:

Wednesday 19.04.1972.... *"Clive (Massey) rang me up at work to say there was room in the car to go and see the Villa play at Chesterfield. Left work at 3.45pm went on the back of Clive's motorbike to Pype Hayes. Then by car to the match. Won 4-0. Brilliant. Home 11.30pm".*

It was a great night out except for the simply terrifying trip on the back of Clive's bike. I had not been a pillion passenger before and have not been since. Four wheels for me every time.

Another special occasion was the 1972 FA Charity Shield. Normally this is played between the winners of the First Division and the holders of the FA Cup. This year both Derby County and Leeds United declined to take part. Manchester City, who finished 4th in the First Division, and Third Division Champions Villa agreed to step up:

Saturday 05.08.1972... *"John and I went down the Villa. Lost 0-1 to Man City in the Charity Shield. Robbed by F Lee penalty".*

I went down to the Blues a couple of times: on one occasion to see them play Everton just after Bernie Wright had moved there although I don't think he got a game that day; the other was a local derby against Wolves which the Blues won 1-0.

WATERFORD CELTIC FC

I played a lot of informal football with the lads in the parks around us but missed the involvement of playing in a proper team after Royal Star finished at the end of the previous year. Mike O'Mahoney from Wragges asked John Clegg and I if we would be interested in playing for his local team. I jumped at the chance. Mike's parents were from Southern Ireland and they were part of a strong Irish community. He played for Waterford Celtic in the Birmingham under twenty-one league. They were quite a decent side and had both a non-playing manager and trainer. We had training sessions on a Wednesday night at King's Heath High School, which we frequently followed with a drink at the Hare and Hounds pub.

There was a slight drawback to training as Waterford Celtic also had a Gaelic football team. I was still growing but had barely reached ten stone soaking wet. The Gaelic footballers were on average twice my size and some of the training routines were, to say the least, challenging! We were often paired up with them and instructed to do piggyback shuttle runs. Fine on the way up the gym with me on top but the return shuttle with a twenty stone gorilla on my back was a killer.

The actual football was much more enjoyable as I settled into a right midfield position. We were unbeaten in our first nine games and I was playing well and scoring goals (eight). Our tenth game was a semi final against Northfield, a good side who narrowly beat us, maybe because I *"didn't play well"*.

Both Mike and I also played for Wragges in friendlies against other firms. In October Roger Mason, one of our qualified

Solicitors, asked Mike and I to play for his team, Wylde Green College Old Boys. They played on Saturday afternoons, which meant it didn't clash with Waterford's Sunday afternoon games, but the calibre of play was not quite what I had become used to:

Saturday 07.10.1972...."*Played centre forward for Wylde Green. Hopeless team lost 7-0. Ref gave me a lift home*".

Roger was a skllful midfield player and although I stopped playing for them for a while, they did get better and I returned a year or so later to play many more games. I was a little injury prone, which led to a couple of visits to A&E. I accepted my injuries as a result of my total commitment to the sport. The first was a splintered bone in my left hand; the other was a sprained ankle. Neither too serious but this was not the end of my football related visits to hospital.

FALSE STARTS WITHOUT SPARKS (Dates which didn't lead to anything)

Diana
Ann Mac' from work was keen for me to meet her friend Diana. Eventually we arranged to go to the Wragge's Christmas do at the Berrow Court hotel Edgbaston on the 7th January. It went well and we got on fine. A couple of days later we met for lunch on 10th January and again on the 12th. After a night at Bogarts on the 13th with John Clegg and Linda, it fizzled out.

Jean
Jean and Pam had been part of our "scene" for the last eighteen months or so but they stopped coming out with the gang after last Christmas. I still saw Jean as I often travelled home from work on the train where Jean was a regular companion. We got on well together and I eventually asked her out at the start of May. She turned me down. I persevered and asked again later in the month, this time with success. It

was short lived, however, as it was clearly not seen by Jean as a "date". Perhaps the choice of a trip to see the film "Mary Queen of Scots" on John's pass did not quite cut the mustard. From then on we still chatted on the train, but just as friends.

Lynn
There was obviously some sort of "hangover" from last year's connection, which started in Skegness as I continued to have occasional contact with Lynn even after the panic ending in the previous autumn. I don't quite know why I sent her a Valentines card. I was probably reacting to her surprise phone call in January when she floated the idea of our groups meeting up for a holiday on the south coast in the summer. She rang me at work a couple of times. Once in response to my card for her eighteenth birthday in April and again in June just for a chat, which lasted twenty minutes. The holiday didn't materialise and inevitably the calls dried up.

Dilys
Dilys and I had known each other for some time. We belonged to groups that crossed over such as the youth meetings at Waterloo Road and the youth club at Yardley church. She was slim with dark hair and attractive features. She was intelligent, as evidenced by getting eight 'O' levels at her first attempt, and appeared mysteriously cool. Many of my friends expected us to get together at some point but I was always unsure. When I did finally take her to see "The Godfather" the evening proved that I should have trusted my instincts. We clearly had lots in common but there was no chemistry.

Sue Kilroy
We had not been to the Sportsman's Arms (resited Rio) for many months but when we returned in December I had a pleasant surprise:

Sunday 10.12.1972…"*went to Sportsman's. Got talking to Sue Kilroy. She goes to Byng Kendrick School*".

Next week:

Sunday 17.12.1972...."*went to Sportsman's. Danced 3 times with Sue Kilroy. She's great*".

I then went down with the flu and was off all week. Next Sunday was Christmas Eve. Guess what?
"Sue not there, has flu"! This story rolls on for a while.

WHAT ELSE WERE THE GANG UP TO IN 1972?

Gaz
It wasn't a good start to the year when he celebrated his seventeenth birthday on 2nd Jan by throwing up on the Sportsman's Arms coach. Like me he was not a big drinker and this was a painful reminder. We thought it hilarious but the coach driver didn't. Gaz's on-off relationship with Fiona continued for a little while, however in May he turned his attention to Glynis (Yes she of Braden's Week and my dumping fame). She dumped Gaz a couple of weeks later but they were soon back together, albeit for a short while. He left school in the summer and went to college. Throughout 1971 I had recorded a number of Gaz's bad moods, although this trend seemed to reduce throughout the year and further improved when he met someone special in 1973.

Bri
There was a sad start to the year when Bri's Dad passed away in January. He wasn't a well man but it was still a huge shock and I knew what he was going through from the loss of my own Dad a couple of years previously. His attendance at Central was not 100% but when the "O" level results came out at the end of August he had passed in three subjects; British Constitution, Art and Geography. He went to work at the stockbrokers where his sister Ann had worked for a while. Bri and I had a go at buying shares when we invested in Rosgill Holdings, one of Wragge's clients on floatation. Insider dealing? Definitely not! Clearly not a wise choice as the shares opened weakly and never improved. In fact, their

biggest contribution was in helping us complete a rhyme for the office cabaret. Sung to the tune of Men of Harlech, "JHD spends all day phoning his golf club and Rosgill Holdings, all his files are merely show, good old Wragge & Co". We sold them at a small loss and put it down to experience.

John L

He was still knocking back the pints on selected occasions although he was usually in control. We often went to the Villa together. His Dad, Arthur, would often come too and provide a welcome lift. His Mum, Doreen was good value and often threatened to throw John's clothes out on the doorstep if he was late home again. She never did. He repeated his 5th Year at Central and added the valuable English 'O' level he was missing. He had several job interviews and I was shocked when I heard he had gone to the Central Fire Station for one. I just could not see him sliding down that pole. Panic over, it was an administration role. He even had an interview at Wragge & Co but decided to join the Nat West where he would stay until he retired 40 years later.

Tez

Tez had a Saturday job at Toft's the Butchers at the Yew Tree before he left school in the summer. It was a natural progression for him to join them full time. Not afraid of hard work, diligent and good with customers he was a "shoe in". Like John he still liked a drink but was nearly always in control or asleep and never caused any trouble when he had a couple.

Shrimp (Paul Wells)

This was the year that he started to join in with the core more regularly We soon realised that he could also hold his own when it came to having a drink. It was Tez who decided that he had "hollow legs". Like Bri, he completed his 'O' level year with two good subject passes in, English and Maths. He left Central but it took him some time to find work that would interest him.

In the Duffin House

Mum had received a very welcome inheritance from Great Aunt Rose in Canada. She shared £2600 and some nice jewellery with her sister, my Aunt Joyce. Mum gave Steve and I £50 each and mine went straight into the Halifax. It also meant we upgraded to a twenty-four-inch TV, still rented from Radio Rentals and still black and white, but it had BBC 2 the home of televised cricket. The money also meant that Mum did not have to work fulltime and instead chose to help out at the playgroup attached to Yardley Parish Church.

She didn't go out much other than to the retired Co-op workers club with her friend, Hilda Reynolds, with whom she had worked before getting married. But she did go on holiday with both Hilda and my Grandad. Grandpa Duffin was a great chap who I loved to bits. Since my Nan had died the previous year he came for dinner with us almost every Sunday. Despite being in his eighties he was fit and had a great sense of humour. He had us in hysterics when he turned up one Sunday to relate the story of how he had stood in line for an hour the previous day only to find he was in the queue for Slade (the band) tickets instead of tickets for the Pete Murray's Open House show. For many years, we had sterilised milk delivered because I didn't like the taste of the normal milk. We called it "stera", he called it "stereo". Bless him.

I don't think my Mum was too pleased when I decided to join the latest trend of home brewing. The kit came from Boots at 35p and promised to make sixteen (delicious) pints:

Wednesday 29.11.1972…"*Mick, John C and I all bought home brew beer kits 35p for 16 pints. At night I made the beer. What a STINK. Borrowed a lot of stuff from Tez*".

Then there was the tasting two weeks later;

Monday 11.12.1972……" *tasted home brew, Great*".

Lies, all lies. It would not be the end of my brewing attempts but if I am honest, I never really liked it and it was a pain to produce.

My brother Steve was doing well at Lloyds Bank and was selected to become a full-time trainer at their Hindhead Training Centre in Surrey for a two year period. Mum and I missed him although he came home quite often at weekends.

We also saw less of the Muddimans. Uncle Peter (my late Dad's best friend) had been fantastic at sorting out Saturday jobs for me but now being in full-time employment this was no longer needed. He could see that my Mum was coping pretty well, particularly after her inheritance, so he took more of a back seat but we always knew he was there if we needed him. Their eldest daughter, Linda, turned twenty one in the Spring;

Sunday 12.03.1972…" *Grandpa came for the day and we all went to Hilda and Pete's in aid of Linda's 21st birthday. She complimented me on my hair style - flattered. Julia didn't seem too good. I enjoyed the gathering".*

Uncle Peter and his son Andrew came to call on Christmas day. Unfortunately, I was, guess where? Yes at the "Ringers" with the gang minus John L who often went out for Christmas lunch.

WHERE HAVE ALL THE PARTIES GONE?

I think a combination of changes led to the number of house parties dropping substantially. The main reason being that people were leaving school and starting work, which disrupted contact. For example, the Ford brothers had both left Central with Mark in Newcastle for many months whilst Paul had gone to University. Those that had started work now had new friends and more money, providing more freedom and more choice.

There were still a couple local parties arranged by the girls who went to the local youth club. There was a slightly embarrassing moment when Ann Turner turned down Gaz's advances at Kate Reilly's party at the end of the year.

Even the traditional Yardley family New Year's Eve party was held two days early on the 29th December. For the first time in a long while I was at home with my Mum as the clock struck midnight and we said goodbye to 1972 and hello to 1973.

CHAPTER 4 1973: Driving forward

At long last the Vietnam War ends and US troops begin to return home. The Watergate scandal deepens but does not reach its full force. In space the first space station is launched by America. Financial markets and economies are hit by an oil crisis.

At home the UK enters the European Union on the 1st of January; Northern Ireland votes overwhelmingly to stay in the UK; the IRA bombs the mainland targeting Central London and even Birmingham. The economy suffers as strikes continue, Value Added Tax is introduced at 10% and inflation reaches almost 9%. British Leyland launches the Austin Allegro with its oddly shaped steering wheel. On the entertainment front the film "Don't Look Now" starring Julie Christie and Donald Sutherland hits the silver screen and Pink Floyd's best-selling album "Dark Side of the Moon" enters the album charts.

NOTHING STANDS STILL AT WORK

It now seems hard to believe but in 1973 New Year's Day was only a bank holiday in Scotland, the rest of the UK had to wait another year to gain the extra day. The first day back saw the office Cabaret team in a panic with the big performance only four days away. It turned out to be *'all right on the night'* helped by a few "*scoops*" (drinks):

Friday 05.01.1973...."*went to Berrow Ct and rehearsed until 5.30pm. Cabaret went off well. Me as Looby Loo. Danced all night. 3pts 6 Sherries! Lift into town and meal at the Bangladesh and back to stay at Mick's. Forgot I had a driving lesson booked (for the morning)".*

In the New Year sales, I splashed out on a new suit from "Archbishops", a trendy men's clothing shop close to our offices, which would now be described as "designer". I loved this three piece with waistcoat even though it cost £26.45, in the sales. I had just been given a £50 pay rise, which eased the pain somewhat.

I had started the year as part of a small team encamped on part of the eighth floor. It soon became clear that this was a very temporary measure in more ways than one. In early January it was announced that over the next few months we would all be moving to brand new offices taking up three floors of Bank House. The tower block was part of the development built to house the regional offices of the Bank of England. Initial sketches of the internal layout were impressive so I decided to take a closer look at one of the floors already occupied to see if it met with my approval:

Thursday 18.01.1972...."*in the afternoon M.o.M (Mike O'Mahoney) and I went to Bank House 5th floor, quite good. We are moving there at the end of the year*".

This was not the only move afoot. With Paul Howard (articled clerk) coming back after recovering from a broken leg a space was needed on the eighth floor.

Friday 02.02.1973... "*JHD told me that I will be moving in to Mr Lawrence's (partner) group. Not too bad*".

Pat Lawrence was I think senior to JHD and I had liked him ever since he had been most complimentary about an essay he had given me to write the previous year. He was confident and had a charismatic presence! I moved down to his group a few days later:

Friday 16.02.1973.... "*Moved to 6th floor right next to PGL's room with a nice new desk. PGL gave me a talk, good. Think we'll get on together*".

Almost straight away I was given a really interesting file that would be with me for months and earn a nice fat fee for the firm. It was for Glynwed Ltd who owned a large amount of land in the Midlands, acquiring it piecemeal over many years. They now wanted to tidy up their 'estate' and register it at the Land Registry. It was like a giant jigsaw puzzle and I have always liked jigsaw puzzles. David Wyndham Smith, a junior partner gave me the file. David was pleasant enough but didn't smile much. We called him "the boffin".

On the gossip front John Clegg was showing an increasing interest in the new office junior, Tina. She was immediately named Tina Bopper (because she was the office teeny bopper). By the end of February they were an item and suffered a considerable amount of teasing from the rest of us. This was ironic, possibly hypocritical, in the case of Mike O'M who took Tina out a few weeks later. John C had just been awarded £200 from the criminal injuries compensation board following an assault in a city centre nightclub and was in a position to show Tina a good time.

I liked working in PGL's group especially as the files were interesting but as the work grew the poor quality of the typing support became exposed. Basically those of us at or near the bottom of the "food chain" lacked dedicated typing support and much of the time we had to negotiate or even plead for help. I was lucky in that I had a lot of help from the two partners' secretaries, Jane and Ann sited in JHD's work group. Ann was JHD's secretary and Jane worked for senior partner, John Keast, who was often out of the office leaving Jane with spare capacity. Jane was now one floor and Ann two floors above me but they still helped me a lot. However, when Ann got married at the end of June my typing support hit a new low:

Wednesday 11.07.1973…*"typing is still useless. Bring back Ann Taylor (*Mrs Newby now*). Due back Monday".*

Love was in the air as on the day of Ann's return from honeymoon I learnt that John and Anne McN' had become engaged at the weekend. Their relationship first blossomed whilst helping with the post shift and they were set to go on to marry and have a family. My days helping with the post were now over but I soon found an alternative way of supplementing my income at work:

Saturday 18.08.1973...*"Arrived at 10am. John C and I worked extremely hard. We moved 2 yrs of DL's (*senior partner David Liddle*) files down to Temple Street".*

With a move to Bank House pending, hundreds of old files were gradually being moved to storage in the basement in Temple St and a similar basement facility on Colmore Row. It was paid overtime and we were left to organise ourselves and have a pint afterwards. This went on for a few Saturdays and occasionally during the working week.

Before I moved to PGL's Group on the sixth floor Mr Keast (Jane's boss) had given me some work concerning the sale of a bungalow owned by a firm in Wales. It was unusual, as the firm owned two bungalows with one mortgage secured on them both. When I completed the requested sale of one of the bungalows I repaid the mortgage and then reapplied for a new mortgage to be secured on the remaining property. WRONG. In my ignorance, I thought this was logical. But there was now a tightening of mortgage funds and this was being treated by the Alliance Building Society as a completely new loan and was rejected due to lack of funds. Was I worried? Yes I was but Mr Keast was brilliant and saved the day with a personal letter to the CEO of the building society and they relented and all was well. I never made that mistake again.

Work fluctuated from really quiet: *"I am completely up to date so I went round to four partners asking for work"* .....to extremely busy: *"seven completions set for Friday"* (27th July). But another pay rise took me to £1200 and made me feel a little better. I don't think I really appreciated the impact of inflation approaching 10% had on the country's standard of living as mine seemed to be unaffected.

As the move to Bank House approached, details were released as to where we would be located. This was great news as I was going to share an office with John Crabtree, a qualified solicitor, on the tenth floor where the rest of PGL's group would be located. I had spent some time with John, as we had both been members of the office cabaret team and I knew we would get on.

We moved on the 1st October. The firm had been in Windsor House for over eleven years having moved from Bennetts Hill, which it had occupied since 1834. Looking back it seems strange that we were moving into such smart premises - planters and all, right in the middle of an oil crisis, increasing inflation and just before the start of the three day week. But I didn't have John's company for long as he moved to an office of his own shortly after the move, swapping with Robert Caddick another qualified solicitor. Unfortunately John suffered with Meniere's disease, which affects the inner ear causing vertigo, tinnitus and hearing loss. I was told that he would benefit from having a *quiet* room of his own!

Apart from now having an office in a swish air-conditioned building, complete with planters, the biggest change was having to be in work on time. I had joined the big boys on the tenth floor and had to act like them, well to some extent. Virtually every day since I joined the firm I had arrived after the scheduled start time of nine o'clock. So few people arrived on time I did not feel compelled to be at my desk much before 9.15am. The move soon changed that. The other big change was the disappearance of Betty and her tea trolley as we now had to help ourselves in the tearoom. It was more effort but at least the spoon no longer stood up by itself and the tea colour had been reduced from a dark orange to a more palatable shade of brown. There were technological changes too. A new phone system made it possible to call direct and even more advanced was the introduction of an early type of paging equipment with the small device vibrating to alert you to call in.

Tuesdays continued to see me attending day release classes but I found it hard to stay to the "*bitter end*" of the evening classes in "*procedure*". We were offered rather generous study leave throughout May and many hours were spent revising. The Law exam was ok: "*good, fair paper, should pass*". The procedure paper on the following day was far more challenging: "e*xam paper very, very hard. Must have failed*". My predictions were 100% accurate and I was naturally disappointed. It was not for the lack of revision this time as I had certainly put the hours in. Missing a lot of the last sessions in college meant that my basic understanding of High Court procedure was lacking and proved decisive. A retake of the procedure paper would have to follow and attending the college evening lectures would also be necessary.

On the work social scene there were a couple of cricket and football matches culminating in an eventful football match against Handsworth Grammar Old boys organised by Colin Cunningham from our billing function who I think was an old boy of the school:

Tuesday 04.09.1973....."*We won 6-3. I scored the first 3. Good game. M.O'M (*Mike) *sent off for fighting. Had a good few (drinks). John Mac took us into town*".

Mike could be a bit feisty on the football pitch. Most of our "friendly" games were against other professional firms such as Pinsents and Eversheds. It was just as well this wasn't one of them and all was well in the bar afterwards.

With my workload, I often had periods when I was looking for things to do and found myself organising sweepstakes for both the Grand National and the Derby. I also found myself volunteering for any collection be it a leaving present, wedding or basically anything.

FRIDAY THE 13TH LUCKY FOR SOME

I did think that my driving test date was a little bit early but my instructor was more confident. When the day for the test arrived I had a lesson at 7.45am -very early for me but necessary as the test was set for 9.05am:

Wednesday 07.03.1973…test *finished at 9.30 FAILED. Unfair; not looking round when moving off,- hand brake on- missed gear on right turn. Put straight in for next one".*

Sounds pretty fair now. My second test date soon arrived as I secured a cancellation. The date (Friday 13th) may have led to the opening up of a test but I was not superstitious, however it didn't start well:

Friday 13.04.1973…*"instructor didn't turn up as he had smashed the blue escort. Bloke turned up in yellow one. Had lesson and PASSED even though I stalled it once. Went back to work".*

The very next day Ann Taylor (JHD's secretary) arranged a visit to the car lot in Digbeth where she had bought an NSU which she was very pleased with. I saw a nice one but it was beyond my limited resources. Nevertheless the search had started only slightly hampered by my complete lack of mechanical knowledge. Most of my friends and even some of their dads matched my mechanical ignorance. A couple of weeks later I looked at a Riley but again it was out of financial reach. Spookily whilst searching I saw our first family car ; a black four door Morris 1000, 9121 WD. It looked in good condition but was not for sale.

Into May and my neighbour Reg Tranter, who lived directly opposite, had volunteered to help with the search. He worked at the British Leyland (BL) car plant and because of this I assumed he had a good working knowledge of cars and car buying. We would soon find out:

Friday 18.05.1973….*"at night bought my first car a 1966 maroon mini MBY 611D (Morris) went with Reg. No bumpers!".*

To be fair we did check to see if it was a legal requirement to have bumpers and it wasn't but perhaps we should have read more into it. We didn't. I think I paid about £150. My first problem was when I tried to change the oil and found it was sealed! I found a way round this problem but it was not the end of my problems. My friend Garf had passed his test just before me and his dad had fixed him up with a smart blue mini that, despite failing its first attempt at an MOT, became a reliable motor and made mine look a bit dodgy.

A couple of days after buying my mini Reg came over with a gift of a pair of seat belts. Reg worked on the area that fitted seat belts and he informed me that BL had just moved over to a new type of belt. The new ones were more comfortable as they moved with you unlike the old fixed type that stayed in the same position. Reg had just fitted the new type to his car, making the old fixed type available to me. However, the new belts puzzled Reg, as he could not understand why you could still move your body forward in them. "How is that going to save you in a crash?" he queried. I suggested we get in his car and drive around the square. Every few yards I said "brake hard!" and the belts locked. "Amazing!" said Reg. "How does that happen?" "IT'S INERTIA REG" I said with glee. And so, he became known from that day forward, as "Inertia Reg".

Just a few weeks later Garf and I were due to drive both our Minis down to the south coast for a week's holiday with John L and Tez. Right up until the week before departure we had planned to go in both cars. However, I sensibly took mine in for a service and asked the garage if it was safe to drive down to Goodrington near Paignton? "I wouldn't drive it past the end of this road" came the reply. This meant we had to rethink our plans and thankfully John L and Tez were kind enough to agree to go down to Paignton on the train *(£5.50 return)* where Garf and I would pick them up.

After deciding not to risk the long drive to the south coast my mini was put up for sale and eventually sold for £120 in November. I was glad to see the back of it and put the whole episode down to experience. I had learnt a lot. First and foremost, you only get what you pay for. Paying very little for a car is not worth the risk. Secondly just because you work at a car plant doesn't mean you know anything about cars, or seat belts.

GOODRINGTON QUAY 23rd June to 1st July

Holiday negotiations started as early as January with the favourite being a return to the YMCA at Torquay. Unfortunately they couldn't accommodate us and we looked at other options in the same area. The final decision was to book an apartment at Goodrington Quay just outside Paignton.

Garf and I set out from home at 3.00am and arrived in plenty of time to pick the boys up from the station and take them to the pub for lunch in Paignton. The weather was excellent and we spent the afternoon in the sea and on the beach. At night we went to the Mermaid Disco (*30p entrance)* where Garf and I paired up with two girls ; Sarah (with me) and Julia (with Garf) - who whisked us off to another disco, The Pacific. Both girls were at college locally so we arranged to see them the next day.

The next morning Tez cooked breakfast and we headed off to the go-kart track where I was fortunate to be given a kart that was faster than everyone else's which made for great fun. In the afternoon Garf and I picked up Sarah and Julia and took them to picturesque Dartmoor. That night we visited three pubs, following their recommendations and local knowledge: Bickleigh Mill, The Church Inn and The Ship Inn.

By Monday the girls were back at college leaving the four of us to entertain ourselves in the amusement arcade where I had some success at bingo. Garf and I picked the girls up from college but Julia told Garf that she had an exam the next day and couldn't come out to play. Amazingly Sarah's mum lent me her brand new mini clubman, which only had 600 miles on the clock which was considerably more miles than I had driven since passing my test just two months earlier. Sarah and I went to The Castle pub in Torquay (which I had visited during our stay last summer). I returned both the car and Sarah safely home and walked back to our apartment, a 45 minute walk, arriving back at the flat at 2.15am. Sarah and I got on well and I was relieved to return the mini in one piece, as I was still a very inexperienced driver.

The boys went into Paignton the next morning to buy and write post cards for home. Having done our 'duty' we then spent a lazy afternoon around the amusements and buying T-shirts for £1.50. At night Julia was free to join us so the four of us went in Garf's mini to the Sea Trout Inn at Staverton, and then on to The Ship Inn, ending up at the harbour to 'chat' until the early hours.

On Wednesday, the girls decided to miss college as they would not be able to go out with us that night. We went to Julia's and spent the day listening to records and just hanging out. At night just the boys went to Penelope's Disco where we had a good laugh as Garf had attracted the attentions of a less than attractive young lady. We were at Penelope's again the following night but this time with Sarah and Julia for 'protection'. We discovered Tez there severely under the influence. I think the over indulgence of amusements had taken their toll.

On what we thought was our last full day of holiday we picked up our bingo prizes, a pair of stainless steel tankards was my reward for too many games, and I am sure they were never used. More pubs were visited with the girls including The Cave Bars as we prepared to say our goodbyes. However, it turned out not to be our last day as Sarah's mum came up trumps yet again and amazingly agreed to Garf and I kipping down at Sarah's on the Saturday before returning home the following day.

We saw John and Tez off on the train and after a good breakfast at Julia's we went into town to say hello to Sarah who had a Saturday job at Boots. Our real last night out was spent back at the Mermaid Disco, where it had all started the previous Saturday. We got up quietly on Sunday morning, said our goodbyes and took our time returning to Brum, arriving home just after 5pm.

Garf and I had a splendid week but I am not sure Tez and John L would say the same. Even now I feel a little guilty but Tez would turn the tables in a similar fashion next summer when the lads venture abroad for the first time.

PAIGNTON TAKE TWO, 4th to 11th August

I am not sure when we decided to go back to the Paignton area for a second holiday but I had kept in touch with Sarah during the five week gap. I had sent her a postcard (not sure what of, maybe the Rotunda!) and she had responded with a letter. We also had one twenty minute phone call. All very relaxed with no pressure on either side. In the intervening weeks she had passed her driving test, which promised to be very useful for possible trips to the pub. The original group for the holiday was Bri, Garf, Tez, Shrimp, Gaz and me. Even though Gaz was now going steady with Chris he was still keen to go. Just a few days before we were due to set off Shrimp pulled out. Fortunately my brother Steve stepped into his place, which meant we also had another car and driver.

Steve hired a VW beetle and we set off on the Friday evening at 9.00pm. Unfortunately it wasn't a good start to the journey as we went several miles down the wrong motorway. Being young and carefree it didn't bother us as we had all night to get to the English Riviera. The other problem was that I didn't take my diary, which means I have to rely on my memory as a record of the holiday.

Our apartment was on the main road through Paignton making it handy but also a little noisy. The first thing we did on Saturday morning was to walk into town and visit Boots where Sarah was working. This didn't go as well as I hoped, in fact that was the last time I saw her. It was always going to be difficult with five other lads in tow and my lack of wheels, but for whatever reason things had cooled and we decided to move on.

We experienced some great weather that week and we took full advantage. We knew that one of the girls from the Ringers, Ann Turner a recent girlfriend of Garf's, would be staying nearby with her family. We looked them up and discovered to our joy that they had a speedboat and water skis. We met up at the beach and had great fun trying our hardest to stay upright with only occasional success. As a thank you we took Ann out for a meal at a decent steak restaurant in town. Memorably Tez made a classic comment. When asked how he would like his steak cooked he paused as if considering his options carefully and then replied, "medium rare, well done". His order was interpreted as medium, and apart from us teasing him all night, the evening was a success.

What we didn't realise until the next morning was how sunburnt we had become whilst playing in the sea. We all suffered but Bri was definitely the worst. Although dark haired he seemed to be quite fair skinned. The following day saw us constantly searching for shade, as it was painful to just be in the sun even when fully clothed.

There were some mixed fortunes during the week. Gaz, with the help of Garf's selection skills, backed three horses which all won and he found himself £26 better off. This was more than enough to cover the cost of his holiday!. Unfortunately, a fair bit of his winnings was spent on 'several' gin and bitter lemons, which left him so ill that at one point when his calling for "Huey" would not stop we seriously considered calling for a doctor. Fortunately, it didn't come to that. We also had a bit of bad luck with keys. On one occasion, we locked ourselves out of the flat and had to climb in through an upstairs window. Worse still was locking the keys in the Beetle resulting in a more expensive outcome. Despite this we returned safely to Brum leaving only four weeks before my third holiday of the summer, this time in Newquay Cornwall.

NEWQUAY WITH THE LAVENDERS, 6th to 13th September

This was one of those gift horses you find difficult to turn down. A cheap holiday, thanks to John L's mum and dad, in a place I had never been to before and with my good friend John L. My theory was that his mum and dad preferred not to leave John at home in case he had wild parties, and of course his mum, Doreen believed he would starve without her to cook for him. Again I left my diary at home but this was no real loss as there wasn't much to record. Newquay is a lovely place but out of season in mid September, like so many resorts, it takes on a different persona.

It was so quiet it made Skegness look exciting. There were just so few people about. We did find a decent pub called The Sailors Arms, and tried the Wig Wam (but no thank you man) disco. We resorted to two main forms of entertainment, golf and tennis. The golf was actually pitch and putt that we played each and every day. The tennis was an early video game called Pong which involved using screen paddles to hit the on-screen "ball" past your opponent. That was the nearest we got to a paddle in Newquay. I assume the name of the game came about by taking the Ping out of Ping Pong thereby just leaving a Pong! To sum up the holiday it was a more relaxing than exciting.

HARDLY A YEAR OF ROMANCE

There were very few parties this year although Ann Turner hosted one on the 6th January, which saw me hook up with a girl called Judy. She was a friend of Gaz's girlfriend Chris and was virtually inseparable from her best friend Sheila. The relationship was blighted from the start when the lads nicknamed her "Clarence" due to the imperfect alignment of her eyes. Which is interesting as I was born with a squint in my right eye. Gaz was very keen for us to progress, mainly due to his liking of going out as a foursome. Partly to please him the four of us went together to The Ringers, Bloomers and even out in Chris's mum's car to The Buccaneer pub near the airport. Really though I think Judy and I were going through the motions to keep others happy and it was over between us before the month was out;

Saturday 27.01.1973...."*Went up Ringers finished with Judy. JC, Bri and I went to the Kashmir for a curry*".

Back at the Sportsman's in February I bumped into Elaine Smith a few times, (No not that one), although she was a Saltley girl and a friend of the other Elaine (Yes that one). Briefly we were more than friends, especially on the coach home, but it was just in the moment stuff!.

I didn't send any Valentine's cards this year, as there was a lack of candidates although I did receive one that I assumed was from Dilys due to the Moseley postmark (near her school).

Out of the blue in June I received a letter from Lynn (Skegness 1971) informing me of her forthcoming engagement. A little young at nineteen but I was pleased for her but It made me "*feel old*".

As far as romance was concerned the real puzzle hanging over from last year was one Sue Kilroy.

KILROY WASN'T HERE

I thought Sue and I had so nearly got it together at the end of last year, particularly as I had chatted to her at the Sportsman's a few times at the start of this year but, alas without progress. I didn't see her again until a few months later when the Sportsman's had returned to it's real home at the Rio:

Sunday 01.07.1973… *"Went to Rio. Sue Kilroy asked me to a Barn Dance"*

Now was she asking me to go with her or just selling me a ticket? Erring on the side of caution I went with friends:

Monday 02.07.1973…."*took Shrimp and Kate to a Barn dance. Sue K spoke to me"*

Yep, she was just selling tickets. Boy was I slow on the uptake, or was I? I still had a nagging feeling that a spark had been ignited and it just needed nurturing.

Wednesday 29.08.1973…"*Went to the Mackadown. Sue Kilroy came up to me and we got chatting. Took home in my car. Talked for nearly 2 hrs. Kissed her goodnight and got home 1.10am"*.

What is going on? Two days later I chatted with her in The Parisian in town and another two days later we saw each other at The Rio:

Sunday 02.09.1973…."*Went to Rio. Sue there. Although I spoke to her I lacked the courage to ask her out. I am confused"*.

Something was uncharacteristically holding me back although I was pretty pleased when two weeks later she bought me a birthday drink and delivered it with a birthday kiss. During the next week we crossed paths and had lengthy chats but still this relationship seemed to be a non-starter:

Sunday 23.09.1973… *"At Rio saw SK. I can't explain to myself or anyone else the attraction but it is there, and strong!"*

Either the attraction was not strong enough or not reciprocated so I decided that was that. I didn't have any further contact with Sue. We started to go to different places and mix in different circles. I convinced myself that she had left town, perhaps to go to college. It was hard to accept that she wasn't interested in me after the time we had spent together, but maybe I was just making excuses for my dreadful handling of the situation. Shame, but Kilroy was not here, and not for me.

FOOTBALL, THE BIG TIME

I was still playing for Mike's Waterford Celtic and the team was doing well and winning matches. in February John Clegg (JC) and I were disciplined for missing a match. Our excuse was that the game was on the other side of town and we had no way of getting there. Despite our protestations we were put on the bench for the next match before being reinstated the following week.

The team had made it to our second semi-final of the season against league leaders Coleshill Town. They were the under twenty-one side of a very good set up that at the time was a "nursery" team for Bristol City. Our management was determined that we would reach the final this year and set in motion their plan. The dressing room rumour was that a "star" player, maybe a young professional, was coming down from a team in the north. Basically, we were to be joined by a "ringer". I am not sure how much of this was true although someone new did turn out for us that day. He probably wished that he hadn't bothered particularly as disaster struck after only five minutes:

Sunday 25.02.1973…*"Lost in the semi final at Wilmot Breeden's ground 5-2 v Coleshill Town. Our goalie was sent off after first goal. Burk".*

That said I must have had a decent game as after the match Mick a guy with the winning team approached me and invited me to train with them at their own floodlit pitch the following week. I can't remember what position Mick had at the club but I do remember him driving me from the Yew Tree to training. He drove like a man possessed and I was terrified! The training went OK and I was selected for their next match. We won by a staggering twenty three goals to nil, with my contribution being a mere five! I was still registered with Waterford Celtic, which meant I played under someone else's name for that match. I had now become a "ringer". However, it was almost the end of the season and I am not sure if it was my performance or my objection to Mick's driving but that was my one and only game for Coleshill Town. It was also the end of my Waterford Celtic appearances.

Earlier in the season I picked up a booking for alleged dissent. I did not agree with the validity of the booking and when the paperwork came through I decided to appeal. Although my challenge was based on not agreeing with the referee, I was also interested to find out more about the procedure. It was almost identical to that experienced by professionals and was to be held at the Midland Hotel in the centre of Birmingham. I paid the £2.00 deposit to ensure I attended:

Monday 07.05.1973…*"At 5.30pm John C, M O'M (witnesses) came to my personal hearing of my booking by the County F A at the Midland Hotel in front of 4 chaps. Out by 5.50 pm".*

I thought it would go in my favour as the referee failed to turn up at the hearing but I had to wait until August for official confirmation that *"no further action would be taken"*.

The season finished but the gang carried on playing for fun at Queens Road Park whenever we could. We were now joined by Tin (Martin Wood), Shez (Rob Sherratt) and Cas (Nigel Casley). We often played against a group of "older" men that we nicknamed "The Pentonville Mob" as some of them should definitely have been locked up. They played hard and not always by the rules but it was great experience and lots of fun.

I didn't go to watch the Villa until the start of the 73/74 season after which my attendance really picked up. I rarely went to away games but in September John L and I made the trip to watch our boys play at Notts County. Unfortunately, our support was rewarded with a 2-0 defeat. That was our first and last away trip of the year. Our home games were a little more rewarding, particularly a 5-0 thrashing of Cardiff City with one of my favourite players Bruce Rioch scoring twice.

BERNIE BOLTS BACK

Bernie Wright's first division career with Everton lasted less than a year and he was transferred back to his old club, Walsall, for £10,000. He was a good friend of John Clegg (JC) and we were soon invited to watch him play:

Saturday 24.02.1973....."*In the afternoon JC and I went to Walsall v Oldham. Bernie scored in a 3-0 win. Had a drink in Directors' bar*".

This was not the last time we went to Fellows Park. The next time we were fortunate to meet a well-known celebrity.

THROUGH THE RINGERS

The Assembly Room at the Ring O Bells saw it all; good moods, bad moods, dating, finishing, laughing and crying. The first month of 1973 saw Shrimp dumped by Kate (although not for long), Gaz asked Chris out to Bloomers, me finish with Judy, and Garf finish with Judy's friend Sheila. Mostly it was good fun with plenty of banter. If you needed a lesson in how to take a joke you just needed to be there. But sometimes things could go a bit too far:

Wednesday 11.07.1973....*"Went up Ringers, Tez cracked up and poured a pint over John L's head. Mighty funny".*

Generally the banter was good humoured and you just had to learn to take it as we all had our turn in the spotlight. We laughed so much and so often.

Wednesday 01.08.1973....*"Went up Ringers and had a real laugh with Tin (*Martin Wood*) and Shez (*Rob Sherratt*) about the Oggad (*a friend of theirs*) I was crying".*

There was a big change at the Ringers on the 7th February and I was "*amazed*" by the introduction of a Wednesday "disco". We thought it wouldn't last but it was still going at the end of the year. I referred to it as "*the so called disco*" and after a few weeks, although it was popular I still hadn't accepted it:

Wednesday 14.03.1973..."*Went up the great (sark) Ringers disco with whole mob. Absolutely packed but I don't like the set up".*

Ok I didn't like it, mainly because it was just a bloke playing records with no dance floor and therefore not really a disco. It did however attract more people some of whom we knew, like Elaine (yes that one) and her boyfriend (later to become her husband) Trevor Clarke known as the "Dog", they soon left when they spotted us. The only thing that put a temporary stop to the disco was a beer strike that initially restricted us to drinking mild and then having to hunt down a pint further afield:

Wednesday 02.05.1973..."*Went to Ringers no disco no beer so went to Yew Tree "(*home of the Rio*).

We also made new friends in the form of "Killer'" and his friend Stuart. Killer was a small but powerfully built chap who had a diverse outlook on life and frequently had us in stitches. Not sure where his nickname came from as he was no more a killer than I was! He worked on a building site near The Swan where a new curved office block was being constructed. He was fascinated by the quality of the internal wooden doors being convinced that they were out of keeping with the rest of the building and would certainly last longer than the building itself!

AWAY FROM THE RINGERS

After the Rio had established itself back in it's rightful home in April we divided our Sunday nights between our old favourite and the Bloomers nightclub located at The Swan. The Rio was familiar territory with lots of friendly faces and only five minutes walk from home; while Bloomers was modern, different, and dare I say, more sophisticated, it was all relative. Bloomers did have "crazy" nights and there was a particularly good turn out on 2nd January for Gaz's eighteenth birthday despite it being a Tuesday. We went there a further dozen times during the year and had plenty of fun nights. It helped that we were not as well known as we were at The Rio. Plus you could dance closely with the girls rather than freak out with the boys!

We went to The Rio twenty seven times during the year as it was just so handy. We all had lots of friends there, and my interest was piqued by the chance of seeing Sue Kilroy. On Fridays and Saturdays we usually ventured into town or went out to pubs in the cars. The Ringers had became a week day meeting place which I went to more than 150 times during the year but I still only drank just over a pint per visit on average. We started to experiment with nightclubs in town such as Sloopy's, Rebecca's, Samantha's and even the Top Rank.

Sloopy's was a small basement club on Corporation Street. I think we liked its cozy, almost intimate, atmosphere. Our first visit proved to be an eventful evening:

Friday 23.02.1973……"*At night John L, John C, MO'M, Tez and I went to Bogart's bier Keller. All drunk except me. Went on to Sloopy's. Tez fell asleep on the floor and John L fell down the subway. Home in taxi 2.30am*".

One of the advantages of Sloopy's was the handy location of a taxi office just around the corner. We only went back a few times before the end of the year but it became our favourite "town club" over the next couple of years.

Rebecca's was a much bigger and more commercial venue on three floors located off John Bright Street. I recollect having a dance with a young lady who asked whether I was doing a "one or a two". I quickly realised she was referring to the moves to each side and I soon adopted the "two" rhythm to match her and all was well. Not exactly "Strictly Come Dancing" but enough to avoid embarrassment. It was not a place we visited regularly although we returned a few times over the years, most notably in 1979, six years later for my stag night.

During the previous year we had a spell of ice skating at the Silver Blades ice rink in Pershore Street. It was now time for us to move upstairs to try out Samantha's nightclub. We were not impressed; "*what a dive*" (16th Mar). I only went back once in the summer because I learnt Sue Kilroy and friends were going to be there after we bumped into them in town one night. Apart from being a "*dive*" it was also a bit out of the centre of town so it was soon crossed off the popular list despite the possibility of meeting Sue there. We also went once – just the once- to the Top Rank. Enough said.

As far as city centre pubs were concerned our favourite was The Parisian, which we visited at both lunchtime and in the evening. It would be an exaggeration to say it had become

The Ringers of town but it was regularly used as our meeting place, particularly at weekends. Other popular venues were The Tavern, Costermonger and a little further out, The Longboat. An increasingly popular lunchtime pub was The Gilded Cage on Stephenson Place below the Palisades shopping centre. The main attraction was the food, which was great value with our favourite egg, beans and chips a real bargain at 21p.

Venturing further afield we had started to visit The Mason's Arms in Solihull High Street, and The Boat Inn at Catherine-de-Barnes. We also went to The Clock on the Coventry Road, which had several, yes, clocks, but absolutely no atmosphere and you certainly couldn't get your beer on tick!

For some unknown reason we had stopped going to concerts. Perhaps familiarity was breeding contempt as we had now seen a lot of bands, several more than once. We did however venture into other forms of entertainment:

Friday 04.05.1973…"*John C, John L, MO'M and I went to Birmingham Hippodrome to see MONTY PYTHON'S farewell tour. Very good. Then to Sloopy's. Then Houseboat for a steak and taxi home*".

That is what I would call a top evening! Interesting that it took more than another forty years for the Python team to really call it a day. The other cultural change can be blamed on John L's mum. She had disappeared from the ABC New Street, as did our free pass. Doreen had settled for more sociable hours working at a menswear shop in the Palisades. Having to pay for the cinema should have made us more discerning but in reality it just stopped us going, except once:;

Wednesday 31.01.1973…"*Went to see" A Clockwork Orange", with John L, John C, Bri, and Gaz. Good*"

Our passion for playing cards, particularly brag, was on the increase and so were the stakes. The favourite venue was still

Tez's because of availability due to his parents being at work most evenings at The Yew Tree off licence. We also played a lot at Bri's and sometimes at mine. We had now expanded into Garf's and even the house of his friend and near neighbour John Hargreaves. The stakes rose along with our earnings. We were all keen sometimes playing both before and after a visit to The Ringers.

Being out virtually every single night restricted my television viewing. I did make an effort to watch a couple of programmes, notably Colditz on a Monday night. I also enjoyed the new comedy "Man About The House" featuring the attractive Paula Wilcox.. One popular series that was loved by many finished later that year:

Sunday 16.09.1973…"*Today saw the end of Follyfoot A great pity. Best programme on television".*

Perhaps a slight exaggeration but it had built quite a following mainly due to the attraction of Dora played by Gillian Blake. It was essentially a children's programme but it was watched by people of all ages. It was rumoured that she received hundreds of proposals of marriage during the series. Sadly she didn't reply to mine (only joking)!

WHAT ELSE WERE THE GANG UP TO?

Gaz started going out with Chris in the January, wooing her with a night out at Bloomers. We were so pleased with this match because Chris made him happy, and we all benefited from that.

Tuesday 10.04.1973…."*Gaz said…."This year so far has been the happiest 3 months of my life".*

As Gaz rapidly became more   serious about Chris, we saw a lot less of him. They came to The Ringers a few times and Gaz was always keen on trying to go out as a foursome. The real surprise was that he still came on holiday to Paignton with the boys in the August.

Bri became seriously ill in March and ended up in East Birmingham Hospital for more than two weeks with, I think, a stomach problem. We all went to visit him and were shocked by his condition:

Wednesday 21.03.1973...*"At night JL, JC, Tez, Killer, Stuart and I went to see Bri. Very bad, drip feed etc."*.

I went again with Steve C a few days later on the 26th when fortunately we found him *"much improved"*. He was discharged on the 4th April and a week or so later he was back in the fold at The Ringers and The Rio. We continued to play cards at his house although he didn't join us in town very often. He was working full time I think at the stockbrokers Smith Keen & Cutler and attending night school. He had been our music guru and clearly influenced our concert attendance, which, without him dried up completely.

Tez was always reliable 'Tez' - a good friend, coming out most nights, and hosting hours and hours of card playing. He provided some memorable moments such as the pouring of beer over John L's head. And, the medium, rare, well done steak.

John L was now working at the Nat West bank in town so I saw a lot of him at lunchtime as well as in the evenings. Trips to The Gilded Cage for their 21p lunches became more frequent. He was still a match for Tez when it came to having a drink, but usually only at weekends. He also continued to be my Villa buddy.

Shrimp (Paul Wells) joined us more particularly on our visits to The Ringers. For much of the year he had an on /off relationship with Kate. He didn't come on holiday with us, probably due to lack of funds, as he had been unemployed for some time. We were both surprised and pleased when he eventually got a job:

Wednesday 15.08.1973…"*Went up Ringers "disco". Shrimp has now got a job, miracle!*"

This may sound a little harsh but lovely lad that he was he had a reputation for being more than a little, shall we say, relaxed. When we were much younger and we used to play "up the field" i.e. Marlborough Cricket Club, we would call for him and his standard reply was "*I'll just put my pumps on*". Often a couple of hours would pass before he sauntered up the road to join us. '*Just putting my pumps on*' became an oft-repeated phrase by us all.

I had my own health issues as I suffered from a series of styes and abscesses. I developed two styes in quick succession in April. The one on my 'good eye' (the left) was particularly inconvenient as the vision in my 'bad eye' (the result of a late diagnosis of a squint) was not great. Although painful, these proved to be mere irritants compared to the abscess in my toe that appeared in the October. My big toe became more and more swollen and as it grew, so did the pain. I had the most horrendous night and my poor mother was reduced to sitting at the end of my bed stroking the underside of my foot to try and mask some of the pain. The things mums do!

The next morning my neighbour, Mr Beresford, kindly drove me to East Birmingham Hospital for treatment. I was anxious and in pain. The medical advice was to cut open and drain the abscess. This was fine by me, anything to get rid of the pain. The local anaesthetic went in and the scalpel approached my now giant toe. Suddenly there was what can only be described as an EXPLOSION OF PUS. It went everywhere! The pus had been under such pressure that it spurted right across the room. But having the pus taken out of me was such a relief. Having the wound packed and redressed wasn't much fun though.

Like most pubs The Ringers sold crisps and I was particularly fond of the salt and vinegar variety. The brand they stocked was "Crispi Crisps" and their slogan at the time was *the crisp that gives you something back on the empties*". Not particularly catchy but accurate as each pack had a token which could be saved towards a gift. I started to collect and I think others in the gang did too, but for me it quickly became almost an obsession. This was partly due to the ridiculous number of tokens required for even a modest gift. I was saving for one of the big gifts; a car rug. I needed hundreds and was soon found scouring the pub for "empties". Even the car park was searched and soggy packets taken home to be dried and relieved of the treasured token. I finally reached my goal, the car rug was secured and we were able to "spread the blanket on the ground" for many years to come.

In July, I had my first experience of "Murphy's" pub (called I think The Moseley Arms) just off Digbeth. Mike O'M's dad, also a Michael, ran a business supplying building labour to major contractors such as Douglas. I think he may also have had an interest in the Moseley Arms as well. They all called it Murphy's, which I assumed was the name of the landlord. This was a real drinkers pub but as friends of Michael senior's son Mike, we were made most welcome. Part of our induction into life at Murphy's was to be introduced to "the hardest man in Birmingham". We were taken into a small room where two strapping men were holding up a frail, wizened old man whose suit had seen better days. We paid due reverence and returned to the main room. We were left in no doubt that this man had once enjoyed a past worthy of note, but his reputation, as the hardest man in Birmingham must have persisted long after his ability to carry it through. Apart from making the acquaintance of 'legends' the only real advantage this establishment had was that in the days when time was called at 10.30pm, the call never came at Murphy's.

At this stage of life, I wasn't really aware of the relative cost of items and the effect of inflation. In 1973 we enjoyed the "Cage" meals at 21p; haircuts at Vic Kent's costing 45p; and high fashion flares at £5.00 a pair. We were all in for a shock over the next couple of years as inflation and prices soared. There were other shocks around the corner as IRA bombs exploded even closer to home.

Little did I know it at the time but big changes lay ahead in 1974.

CHAPTER 5 1974: Life changing decisions

The major news story in 1974 was the resignation of American President Richard Nixon following the Watergate scandal. The global recession hits economies across the world including the UK where inflation reaches 17%. A three day week is introduced and in a tough budget the basic rate of income tax is raised to 33%. The IRA increases their bombing campaign across the country and close general elections are fought in February and October.

In sport, Germany wins the World Cup and Ali beats Foreman in the "Rumble in the Jungle". Manchester United are relegated to the second division. Don Revie replaces England Manager Alf Ramsey whilst Bob Paisley takes over from Bill Shankly at Liverpool.

The entertainment world sees Abba win the Eurovision Song contest with Waterloo. Tom Baker becomes the fifth Dr Who and Monty Python ends. Lord Lucan disappears following the murder of his children's nanny and McDonalds opens its first UK outlet in London. The big local news in Yardley was the introduction of "one man" buses. We also had a visit from Ted Heath at the Yew Tree during the General Election campaign.

The year begins with the usual family and friends' party down at Vicarage Road with the Yardley family but this year saw a first;

Tuesday 01.01.1974...."*Arrived home at 4.30am from the Yardley's party. Good time had by one and all. Had haggis for the first time*".

It may have been the usual start but this year would lead to major changes in my life.

FROM WRAGGES TO "RICHES"

The British economy was in a bit of a mess with a major recession and the miners on strike. This resulted in a three day week to save power, starting on the 3rd January. Our office hours altered to an 8.45am start and a 3.30pm finish. I was pretty ignorant of the effect this was having on the business coming into the firm, which meant I continued to be frustrated by the highs and mainly the lows of work. I was even considering venturing further afield;

Monday 07.01.1974...."*I am still thinking of doing VSO (*voluntary service overseas)".

It soon wore off. Partly due to a pay rise (*now £1300*). Later that month, I lost one of my typing assets when Jane Woodman left and this unsettled me again. Looking after the firm's library made me a suitable candidate for a legal job at GKN, which included managing their legal department's library;

Tuesday 26.02.1974..."*went to Pertemps* (recruitment agency*) last night for a job I saw in the Evening Mail. GKN legal Dept £2000 pa. Have an interview on Friday".

Thursday 14.03.1974...."*heard from Pertemps, I didn't get the GKN job because I was TOO experienced!".

I was really bored and even resorted to bizarre distractions;

Friday 22.03.1974....."*Did some work today but ALL afternoon we had a rubber band war. Great laugh!".

There was some new work including the purchase of a petrol station for Chris Hughes (partner) for £95k, big bucks for me. There was other news as I was told I was on the move to the floor below to work for one of the senior partners, James Whiting-Smith, sharing an office with one of the qualified solicitors, Kevin Garner. I was used to change by now and sharing with Kevin was more useful experience. This didn't stop me looking at other opportunities and the next one would mean a possible move to the seaside;

Saturday 06.04.1974….."*arrived in Weymouth at 1015. Booked into the hotel and went for a walk. Hockey team staying. Played brag won 25p".*

Monday 08.04.1974… *"Had an interview at Batten & Co at 9.15am until 11am. Good job, own room, varied work. Chris Thompson (partner) drove me to their Yeovil office to have lunch with other staff. Very impressive. Home 9pm".*

I had also arranged to see another firm in the afternoon, which I had to cancel. I had planned to claim the travel expenses from both firms to cover my two nights in the hotel. Best laid plans and all that! Two weeks later they came back;

Tuesday 23.04.1974…."*heard from Weymouth. Offer £1600 (£300 more). I am not going. Very bored at work".*

When I got back from Weymouth my Mum's best friend, Hilda Reynolds (the one she worked with at the Co-op in her youth) sat me down and asked me not to leave home yet as Mum would be on her own with Steve working away. This was a factor but I just didn't fancy leaving home and friends yet.

May saw another rise to £1400 but inflation was on the increase too. I began revising for my outstanding exam as soon as study leave became available and was determined to polish this one off to complete my Associateship.

The economic situation and a 'hung parliament' caused some uncertainty, which was seen by increasing turn over of staff. Mike Wooldridge (AKA Muck Spreader) and my room mate Kevin, both left in May. Mike had become a friend by now and was off to work for the Council as he saw few prospects at Wragges. Kevin was off to private practice in Coleshill. As a result, my workload increased with the inheritance of all Kevin's files;

Wednesday 12.06.1974....*"today was the hardest I have ever worked since I have been at Wragges. Did 30 min tape".*

The next day was the start of the 1974 World Cup and I arranged a completion in Solihull to enable me to get home for the 4pm kick off. The next morning JWS told me off for leaving early, which was a bit harsh as it was just effective planning. Such actions simply reinforced my view that I should move on. But there was some good news as I passed my exam and was now an Associate of the Institute of Legal Executives and JWS presented me with a cheque for £50.

I was now on the books of a couple of recruitment agencies and when I returned from my holiday I was offered a strange interview;

Wednesday 24.07.1974...*"went for an interview at a fork lift truck company for a sales position. What a laugh".*

I had a hard time from the two chaps interviewing me, quite rightly, as I had not looked at their products and their frustration was obvious. I should never have been there but it was a very good lesson in the need for interview preparation which would come in useful at my next interview;

Thursday 19.09.1974....*"went for an interview for a Salesman with the Wellcome Foundation. £1720 plus company car a Ford Cortina. Promising".*

Wow! I wasn't really looking for a 'Sales Rep' job but this sounded really good. The company was sound and the training appeared excellent, but there was a niggle. They went out of their way to stress the need for mobility but I was still delighted to receive an offer of employment a few days later.

The next step was the medical with my own GP, Dr Lloyd. It was all going well until the hearing test. He told me to move to the back of the room. He then whispered to me and like a fool I fell into the trap of whispering my reply, which he couldn't hear. I passed however, I wrote and asked for clarification of the mobility question. They confirmed that after about a year's training in the Midlands area I would be allocated my own sales area but it could be anywhere in the country. I decided to seek advice;

Monday 30.09.1974...."*spoke to Marjorie (*my new room mate replacing Kevin) *and Roger Mason, (*solicitor and football player)*. Second thoughts".*

At the same time as applying to the Wellcome Foundation I had applied to the Leeds Permanent Building Society for a Management Trainee position;

Monday 07.10.1974..."*at 10.30 went for an interview at the Leeds PB Soc. Looks very promising. 25 applicants but I got on very well".*

This was the clincher. I was unsure about the Wellcome sales job and the Leeds role sounded more like me. The very next day I wrote to Welcome declining the offer and "*hoping to get the Leeds job*". A second interview soon followed;

Tuesday 22.10.1974..."*went for interview at Leeds PBS. Think I have got the job at Acocks Green branch".*

Wednesday 23.10.1974...." *the manager of the Acocks Green branch, (*Trevor Jones)*, rang me at work to tell me I had got the job subject to a medical and references. I told JWS but he would not accept my notice until next Monday (28th October)".*

The following Monday JWS tried to persuade me to stay by offering to match the Leeds pay. He also said "*I was popular"* and they saw me as a future Fred Preece. That sealed it. Fred was a lovely, knowledgeable chap but one look at him sitting quietly smoking his pipe was not how I saw my future.

I passed the medical by more than a whisper and a start date of Monday 2nd December was set. There were things to tidy up before I left, such as the Glynwed registrations. I saw my fee earnings for the first nine months, which had reached £7000, more than five times my annual salary. With John Mac now at Law school and Mike O' M also leaving it was time to move on.

My roommate Marjorie kindly invited me to dinner with her and her husband on the night before my last day (21st November). They lived on the other side of town and we spent a very nice evening over a splendid meal. Marjorie's husband gave me a lift into town but the police, due to a major incident turned us back. The whole of the centre of town was sealed off after two bombs exploded in the Tavern in the Town and Mulberry Bush pubs. Twenty one people lost their lives in the IRA atrocity. The Tavern was a pub we used and I was in there with John Clegg just days before. There was shock and anger throughout the whole city. The next day was my last at Wragge & Co;

Friday 22.11.1974…"*at dinnertime no one would go to the pub so I bought some drinks which we had in the tea room. I was given an umbrella (£7.35)*".

it was a very strange ending to my time at Wragges. I had started there just before my 18th birthday and left just after my 21st. In many ways this was my "university". I learnt so much and it was tremendous preparation for my future career in financial services. I had much to be grateful for. The decks were now cleared for the real "main chance".

STILL LOOKING FOR THE RIGHT ONE

Denise Wood

Denise was Tin's (Martin Wood) younger sister and I think I met her for the first time when he brought her to the Rio at the beginning of the year;

Sunday 13.01.1974…"*went to the Rio. Spent the whole evening talking to Tin's sister Denise. Took her home and asked her out to the Ringers on Wednesday*".

Wednesday 16.01.1974…"*went to Ringers with Denise. Decided to go to Benidorm, Spain with Steve C and Tez*"

We weren't off to Spain that evening of course but the lack of any other comment spoke volumes. We obviously weren't suited and two days later when Denise phoned we decided to call it a day.

Chris Butlin

No she didn't wear a red coat but our brief encounter was a little out of the ordinary. We met at a rare party and she made the entire running;

Saturday 25.05.1974…."*Went to John Hargreaves's party. I was picked up by Chris Butlin. She asked me out. Also the police came*".

I have no idea why the police turned up but as I did not elaborate it must have been noise or something similar. I don't think I was too keen as I arranged to take her into town on a Monday night, which was usually a sign of being unsure and keeping the meeting under wraps;

Monday 03.05.1974…"*at night went out with Chris Butlin. Went to Cabin and Pen and Wig. Not sure*".

Well that was that. The choice of two very ordinary pubs on a Monday night plus the "not sure" comment added to the realisation that there were no free holidays on offer sealed her fate. There was no further contact (no Hi-de-Hi)

Barbara Jennings

Barbara worked at Wragge & Co as a shorthand typist. She was athletically built as she was a keen runner and, I think, a member of an athletics club, possibly Birchfield Harriers. She lived on the Chester Road just a few doors from where my Aunt Joyce and Uncle Cyril had previously lived before moving to the Isle of Man in 1969.

Barbara and I always got on and both suffered a little teasing from those who thought we should be an item. As my leaving date drew closer so did we, but she had a boyfriend which stopped us progressing apart from a rather 'interesting' journey home on the upper deck of an empty 53 bus. I had to get off near to Stechford police station, as this was not my bus!

On the day I left Wragges, we agreed to go to the Christmas do together a couple of weeks later but she telephoned to say she had suddenly fallen ill on the day. I understood.

KEEPING SHEILA IN THE DARK

In the six months or so that I had a "thing" with Sheila I never got to know her second name. It was a very unusual "affair". When we first met up in the nightclub I thought it was just a bit of fun for one evening;

Saturday 12.10.1974…"*went to Parisian then Sloopy's. Got off with Sheila*"

That was all I wrote and didn't expect to see her again. Admittedly it was dark in there but two weeks later:

Saturday 26.10.1974…"*went to Parisian and Windsor. Then Sloopys. Got off with Sheila, again!!!*".

The two week gap soon made sense as I learnt that Sheila had a steady boyfriend who played semi- professional football. This meant he had to travel quite a distance for some games, so when he was playing away she was too! I should have asked for a fixture list to avoid wasted trips to the club when he was playing at home, but there were other things to consider. The meetings went on for several months until the end of the season the following May.

After a couple of meetings my Mum commented on the amount of make up that my "friend" wore as most of it seemed to end up on my shirts and was not easy to remove. Worse still, I was horrified to come home one Saturday covered in "love bites". This was really worrying, not only as this was a little immature but also because we always met in Sloopy's in the DARK. It made me think that those fangs were real. I was saved by the end of the football season and the garlic I always had in my pocket from then on, just in case!

A SPORTING YEAR

Squash

John Clegg and I had joined the new North Birmingham Squash Racquets Club near Sutton Coldfield towards the end of the previous year. It was not cheap and we had to work hard to get full value, as the club was not easy to get to without a car. It was easier going straight from work. I played all comers, especially if they had a car. It was a new sport for all of us leading to lots of welcome requests for a match.

In addition to JC I played against my brother Steve, Tin, Steve C and Bernie Wright and club members in the squash ladder. I took to it quite well and had a win ratio of about 75%. When I took on the super fit professional footballer Bernie Wright I won the first couple of games due to the fact it was his first ever game, but he soon got the hang of it and put me to the sword. I had a positive record against the two Steve's and JC, which would not carry on into the tennis season.

Tennis

JC was a positive influence on my involvement in sport as we signed up with the local Co-op sports club in Barrows Lane, just round the corner from the Ringers where my Dad had previously been the club secretary. We joined to play tennis but also used the bar and had an occasional game of table tennis. My record at tennis was virtually the reverse of squash. I lost every time to Steve C and took only three matches of the eight played against JC

Ten pin bowling

We also started to play ten pin bowling at Stirchley. It was a bit of a fad and I was not very competent. It was a bit like ice skating the previous year and we never really treated it seriously, but we gave it a go.

Football

I was still very keen to turn out on the football pitch. I played occasional games for Steve C's work team; Farmiloe's and also his other team The Wanderers for whom Tin also played. Wragges also continued to challenged other professional firms. .

Towards the end of the year I decided to go back and play for Roger Mason's team, Wylde Green College Old Boys. I had previously played just one game for them a while back. I had a great start scoring six goals in the four games in the run up to Christmas, and winning all four matches. I would go on to play many more games for them and score lots more goals. Bernie

Wright was now back in the fold at Walsall and JC and I went to watch him play and meet a celebrity;

Tuesday 02.04.1974...."*At night JC and I met Poge George (JC's school friend and occasional Rio attendee). Went to Walsall to see Bernie play. He scored in 2-2 draw v Watford. Stayed for a drink with the players. Elton John (Watford director) bought us all a drink. Then to Sloopys, free entrance with Roger Fry (Walsall player)*".

I went down the Villa a dozen or so times with John L and even went to an away match;

Saturday 26.01. 1974...."*Set off with John L, Pete O and his bro' plus others at 9.20am. Arrived at Arsenal at 12.45pm. Great mob, 5,000. Great match 1-1 leading 0-1 until 65th min. Home 7.30. Went up Ringers*".

We went to the replay at Villa Park a couple of weeks later, which Villa won 2-0 in front of a crowd of 48,000. The Cup run didn't last as we were beaten away at Burnley in the next round and it was back to life in the second tier (Division 2). Things picked up following the appointment of Ron Saunders as the new Manager in June and John and I were regulars in the following season that saw Villa promoted to the top division.

TWO'S COMPANY... 24th June to 8th July

It was back in January that Steve C, Tez and I decided to venture to Spain for our first boys holiday abroad. Three is an odd number but I suspect the cost at £79 kept the numbers down. This was to be my first trip on an aircraft and only my second trip outside the UK, (not counting the Isle of Man). The other was a week long school trip to Paris in 1967. It did nothing for my French as I came bottom in the end of year exams with my teacher (Brian Firth) commenting; "cheerfully incompetent".

After an early start, we arrived at the Hotel Monaco in the resort of Benidorm before midday. It was pretty much as the brochure had described except for one added bonus, it had a TWENTY FOUR HOUR BAR!

Saturday 24.06.1974...."*Hotel very good. Went straight in the pool. At night meet some English birds in Dick Turpin's. Went back to their hotel for a dance*"

We arranged to meet them the following evening but we had not taken account of having to negotiate our way through the twenty four hour bar. Of course we didn't, well not for quite a while. I have no idea how long we spent in the bar but I do remember the after effects;

Sunday 25.06.1974...."*Woke up and felt bad. Terrible hangover. I was sick once and stayed in bed almost all day. Never again*".

Steve and Tez were in a similar state and despite several attempts to get up, the day was a write off.

The next day the beach beckoned, as did the pool resulting in some minor sunburn, but the holiday was off and running. We risked going to the girls' hotel in the evening but it was soon clear that we had fallen out of favour. We moved on to the Istanbul disco. The next couple of days saw a similar pattern of pool and beach with added advantage of discovering an English cafe which was open all hours, *"Susan's"*. By the end of the first week there was a party atmosphere in town;

Saturday 29.06.1974..."*went to celebration dance of Saints Day. Got chatted up by two Spanish birds. Then went ten pin bowling*".

Two days later Steve and Tez focused again on the local girls and I didn't;

Monday 01.07.1974....." *at night went to the Manilla bar. Steve and Tez got off with two Spanish birds. I went around with three lads from Brighton. Went to Susan's then went to the Istanbul disco. Met bird".*

If I remember the young lady in question I got to the exit and ran away. I will put it down to a reaction of being left out by the boys. Two's company and all that. Much of the remaining time was spent lazing by the pool as the boys were off with the girls, but we did have a couple of excursions to complete. It should be borne in mind that we were innocents abroad and therefore our reactions were a little over the top;

Granada Club floor shows, "*fantastic*", Donkey ride, "*very good*", and the inevitable Barbeque, "*fantastic*".

Despite being on my own for some of the time the holiday was a success. The introduction to fabulous weather and plenty to see and do at affordable prices was an eye-opener. I loved swimming and snorkeling in the sea and being able to eat, drink and be merry at any time of the day or night was most appealing. What I now find hard to believe is that just four weeks later I was enduring the British weather in Skegness AGAIN.

SKEGGY ONE LAST TIME 10th to17th August

Hardly the Med' but at least we were an even number this time. This was a third visit for John L and I but for Shrimp and Bri it was their first. Had Skeggy changed since my last visit? Well not really. No groups of girls and no Spanish weather but we made the most of it. We used all the sports facilities as best we could but the biggest difference was at night. This week would see my one and only venture into the world of wrestling;

Tuesday 13.08.1974...."*At night went to wrestling. Les Kellett, fair. Went to Bier Garten, rubbish".*

Well it was something different and we had a laugh at some of the audience taking it all a bit too seriously especially with some of the old dears aggressively approaching the ring with umbrellas at the ready. Les Kellett was almost sixty (born 1915) and it showed but he went on wrestling until he retired just before turning seventy. We had a couple of good nights out; the first to see a band that had a well known hit in the sixties;

Sunday 11.08.1974…."*At night went to the fair then to the Bier Garten to see the New Vaudeville Band, Very good. Shrimp sick in TV lounge".* (hollow legs temporarily out of action!).

Winchester Cathedral was their one hit back in 1967, reaching the top ten in the UK and number one in America. It also won a Grammy Award for best contemporary song. We knew we were taking a bit of a risk with our next choice;

Wednesday 14.08.1974…."*At night went to the Variety Bar to see Bernard Manning 50p. Very good, but dirty. Got John and I as we walked past".*

The lesson we learnt, was that, when watching a comedian, do not to leave your seat unless you want to risk abuse on the way back. Bernard Manning was not exactly PC but he could tell a joke. He would struggle in today's world but was popular back then. We did revisit some of our previous haunts such as the Chuck Wagon before seeing a couple of films on the last two nights. First was "*The Three Musketeers*" which had a fantastic cast including Frank Finlay, Richard Chamberlain and Faye Dunaway. My favourite was Roy Kinnear who sadly died after falling from his horse whilst making another Musketeer film in 1988. On the last night we went to see;

"*Battle for the Planet of the Apes, fair before a final visit to the Ship Inn".*

So ended my third and final visit to Skeggy leaving me with lots of happy memories.

PAUL THE BUILDER (At the National Exhibition Centre)

By the summer Tez had been at Tofts the butchers for over three years and although he enjoyed the work, the money was not great particularly when compared to labouring on a construction site. Tez learnt from Mike O'M that he could work for his dad Michael senior for £1 an hour which was more than double his current wages. The offer was too good to miss and Tez handed in his notice towards the end of June. The labouring work was at the site of the new Exhibition Centre (NEC) close to Birmingham Airport (then known as Elmdon). The main contractor was Douglas and Michael O'M senior provided a number of workers each day. Many of these men came over from Ireland and were directed to "Murphy's" pub in Digbeth where they would find work through Michael O'M. We heard many stories about these new recruits. One stand out tale was the instructions given for their first day by some of the pub regulars. This included the need to make a good impression on your first day so wear your best suit. I am not sure how many took this advice. Tez did not fall for this on his first day but;

Monday 05.08.1974…"*Tez missed the van to take him to the site by standing on the wrong side of the road*".

Not quite sure how this happened but he soon settled into his new life at the NEC. He was however somewhat accident prone and when unhooking a trailer he didn't realise he was on a slope and as the trailer moved backwards he found himself pinned against the wall behind him. No serious damage, thank goodness. He was lucky again when he fell in front of a vehicle and was run over. Fortunately, it was on soft sand so he sank quickly and his legs were just bruised. He continued this line of work for a couple of years before returning to a long career in the butchery trade.

At virtually the same time as Tez started, Mike O'M asked John Clegg and I if we wanted to earn a few extra pounds by working at the NEC for four hours on a Saturday morning. The pay was the same as Tez's i.e. £1 per hour, nearly double our pay at Wragges. One of the reasons for asking us was that some of the regular workers liked to have a drink on a Friday night and have the weekend off. Michael senior was paid by a simple head count so we could stand in. The only problem with this was we hadn't got a clue what to do on site. The first couple of weeks were fine as we were back filling, i.e. moving soil to behind a fence around the lake that only required the ability to use a spade.

The best part of the morning was the breakfast provided in a portakabin. Although it was summer we tried to stay in there as long as we could. One of our next tasks was to dig out circles where trees would be planted in what would be the huge car parks. It was not as simple as it sounds as the circles had to be made in the hard core. Suffice it to say ours were not exactly symmetrical. It was annoying to see all the trees removed at a later date to increase the car park capacity.

After a few weeks JC and I found ourselves isolated from our group and the Douglas supervisor took us off to lay some huge pipes. It was obvious that we were quite literally out of our depth and that was the end of our short construction careers.

NOT GOING DOWN TO RIO

Our visits to the "Rio" dried up with my last night at the end of March, "what a bore". It was time to move on as we had stopped going to gigs and this affected our music interests. In addition, "Bloomers" had become a more attractive venue. There had been some great nights at the Rio over the three and a half years but we were "freaked out". "Bloomers" was now a regular Sunday night out for the boys and I was there more than twenty times this year.

"Sloopy's" was still our main club venue in town with over twenty visits, but we did try the new "Snobs" club in August that I described as *"very smart".* We were so impressed we looked into becoming members but were put off by the £5 fee. The "Opposite Lock" on Gas Street also impressed. We went there a couple of times to support the Law Students wine and cheese parties. Another new place was the "Young Professionals Club", located above shops just off New Street. We had one memorable night at "Barbarella's" when we saw the dance troupe from Top of the Pops, "Pans People". It was hot in there and so were they!

Our local pub was still the good old "Ringers", which I went to over seventy times during the year. It was still our regular weekday meeting place. We also frequented the "Yardley Arms" and the "Yew Tree" (home of the Rio), going to each about a dozen times. The "Yardley Arms" was not far from the "Ringers" and OK for a change, but the "Yew Tree" was just handy. Bri took a part time bar job at the "Manor House", Stechford (formerly the Bull's Head) and we supported him there on half a dozen occasions. In town, the "Parisian" was our number one choice with thirty five visits. While the "Tavern"" clocking up a dozen visits.

There was good news on the film front with the return of the free pass through John L's Mum. We saw some excellent films notably a *"very good"* "Don't Look Now" paired with the "Wicker Man" in February. Next was the *"excellent"* "The Sting". More disturbing was "the Exorcist" which I went to see with my brother Steve; *"very strong emotions".* It was that really creepy voice that sent a shiver down my spine. "Chinatown" was less impressive. The year ended with three *very good* war films; "The Odessa file", "The Dirty Dozen and "Mash". Welcome back the free pass.

Back at home, my Saturday mornings were brightened up by the launch of TISWAS (Today Is Saturday Watch and Smile). The main presenters were Chris Tarrant, Lenny Henry, the attractive Sally James plus Bob Carolgees and Spit the dog. It was meant for children but I was an appreciative viewer.

Another new series was the excellent "Porridge" starring Ronnie Barker. Another enjoyable comedy was aired, "Rising Damp" featuring Leonard Rossiter. I had enjoyed "Colditz" since it started in 1972 right up to the finale in April. Also ending was "Monty Python" after a five year run and "Steptoe and Son" after fourteen years. I made a note of my Christmas Day viewing which was made all the more enjoyable by the arrival in October of our first colour television:

Thursday 25.12.1974…."*Lovely dinner as usual. Watched TV for the rest of the day; The Generation Game, Some Mothers Do Ave 'Em, Mike Yarwood, Morecambe and Wise, Bridge Over the River* Kwai"

Very little happened on the music front. No concerts but there were a couple of unusual album purchases; Dvorak's "New World Symphony" and Stevie Wonder's "Innervisions". I was broadening my musical influences but stayed loyal to Elton John with the purchase of "Caribou".

During the quiet times at Wragges I had began to read a few books. I started with "One day in the life of Ivan Denisovich" by Solzhenitsyn. Not exactly light reading but I enjoyed it. Next was the far lighter "Summer of '42", and saw me devour "*250 pages in less than a day*".
I turned to thrillers next with "*Day of the Jackal*" by Frederick Forsyth. At home I was working my way through Spike Milligan's war memories starting with "Adolf Hitler: My Part in his Downfall."

KEY OF THE DOOR

This was the year that some of us turned twenty one. For a few years it had become the practice to celebrate reaching eighteen, the age of majority. We never missed the opportunity to have a good time and celebrated both eighteen and twenty one. First to reach the magic number was Mike O'M in February. A popular venue for such celebrations was "King Arthur's Court" on Gas Street in the centre of Birmingham. It provided medieval banqueting at a cost of £3.60 per head and was good fun;

Friday 22.02.1974…"*At night Mike O'M, Emanon (*Mike's brother*), John C, John L and I went to King Arthur's Court to celebrate M.O'M's 21*st*. Good. Had a good laugh in town with "spoons".*

The wooden spoons were part of the banqueting equipment that turned into a game of spoon "tig" across town. We had downed a few cups of mead to help fuel the contest. Twenty one going on twelve!

It was John C's turn next to decide how to mark the day. He chose the nightclub Pollyanna's after stopping off for a beer or two at the Tavern. There was a good turn out as our usual group was supplemented by some of JC's old school pals; Martin Winmill, Billy Atkins, and Jim McClenaghan. It was a good night despite the absence of any spoons. In the club I bumped into Ann Jackson (Saltley girl who never returned my tie in 1970). Still no sign of the tie! Come September it was my turn. At home I had sixteen cards and £17 in cash and vouchers. I don't think I did much at work;

Tuesday 17.09.1974…"*Folks at work bought me a smart Papermate pen and a £2.50 record token. About 30 of us went down the Parisian where I spent £5. Then took cakes back for the whole office. At night Steve (*brother*), Steve C, Gaz, Tez, Shrimp, JC, Bri, Tin, Shez went to the Cresta club to see* *(comedian and impersonator) Aiden J Harvey V V good. Then to the Eastern Moon for a curry.*

Cakes for the whole office! I must have been in a very generous mood. It is interesting that I also went to the Parisian at lunchtime on my eighteenth birthday. I remember Aiden J Harvey performing his Peter O'Sullivan impression using his fingers to "canter" on the microphone. A very good night that stands out in my memory.

The last one that year was Tin (Martin Wood). He was in his last year at Bath University where he was studying for a business degree. I was invited to his party in Bath along with Steve C and Shez (Rob Sherratt) travelling in Peg's car (David Yates). We travelled down on the day after the Birmingham pub bombings, which was also the day I left Wragges. Tin was living in Freshford, a village six miles south east of Bath, which I described as "*smart*". The next evening, we went to another twenty first party and didn't hit the hay until 4.30 am. An enjoyable weekend after a very eventful week.

WHO WAS OUT?

The core gang was out in force as usual with Tez, John L and Shrimp (Paul Wells) all making well over one hundred appearances in my diary during the year. Shrimp seemed to be unaffected by losing his job in August as he still turned out regularly and he bought his first car in November. John Clegg fell just short of the ton. Gaz was now spending most of his time with Chris, which meant he fell into the second tier along with Steve C around the seventy mark. Bri only made thirty six outings, probably due to his bar work at the "Manor House". Tin and Shez were out quite often at just under thirty, mainly at the "Ringers" and "Bloomers". The surprise is Garf who only registered two appearances.

When we were not out, the cards were still on the table with over thirty sessions played. Brag was still our chosen game and I was £20.07 ahead for the year, with my biggest win amounting to £4.50

JOIN THE LEEDS AND YOU'RE SMILING

On leaving Wragge & Co I decided to take a week off before starting at the Leeds on the 2nd December. I didn't do an awful lot until later in the week;

Thursday 28.11.1974...."*Went to my new job and spent an hour and a half at the branch. The manager Trevor, and two girls, Sue and Chris very friendly. Sue smart. I think I will be happy there*".

Things seem to happen during my first week in a new job. At Wragges it was a hangover that prevented me going to work on the Friday, but it was different this time. After a series of styes earlier in the year I now had an abscess on my back that was very painful;

Wednesday 04.12.1974...."*Went to work then to doctors who sent me to hospital. Had to wait until 3.30pm for anaesthetic. Didn't feel a thing*".

Brave little soldier that I was I went to work the next day;

Thursday 05.12.1974...."*Went to hospital to have my abscess dressed. The pain was incredible when the dressing was removed and I nearly passed out. Got to work at 10.40am*".

It wasn't long before I discovered that my new boss liked a drink or two;

Wednesday 11.12.1974...."*Very quiet day at work .All afternoon it was just me and Sue. Trevor came back steamed* (drunk)".

I had only been there a couple of weeks but I was delighted to be invited to an informal Leeds "do". A number of staff from different branches in the area had decided to go to Bloomers;

Friday 13.12.1974....."At night went to an informal gathering of 11 Leeds staff. Went to the Swan then Bloomers. Good time danced for ages".

This was where I first met my very good friend Andy Bates. He was at the Sheldon branch just a mile or two from me at Acocks Green. We got on famously and still do over forty years later.

The branch employed a cleaner who appeared each evening just before we closed at 5pm. Mrs Edmonds was a one off. She was cheerful, friendly and very generous. Every Friday she would dish out an array of chocolate bars and sweets. It seemed above and beyond normal generosity but we didn't like to offend and pocketed them eagerly. As Christmas approached, she appeared one evening with a bottle of sherry. Sue and I were getting on well and decided to open the bottle as soon as we closed;

Thursday 19.12.1974....."The cleaner, Sue and I stayed for a drink of sherry. Sue and I steamed (drunk). After the cleaner went we stayed until 8.30pm. I asked her to Bloomers on Christmas Eve and she said yes".

During the next couple of days Sue and I were having fun at work even "*playing foot tig*". Leading me to record; "*we get on great*".

It all looked good for taking Sue to "Bloomers" on Christmas Eve, but things did not go according to plan. For a start, I only had one ticket, which I had bought prior to asking Sue. I tried to buy another ticket but was told I had to try on the night, "*now in a mess*".

Fortunately, I managed to get a ticket on the night so it started off well. We seemed to have a good time but when it came to midnight my advances were discreetly halted. That wasn't all, as when Sue dropped me off I managed to trap my seat belt (not an inertia one) in the door causing it to refuse to close properly. Sue seemed to take it quite well but it appeared to affect her sense of direction;

Tuesday 24.12.1974...."*Sue gave me a lift home and I broke one of her doors. She went round and round the square a few times by mistake and then turned the wrong way on Stoney Lane*".

I summed the evening up;

"I don't think we will make anything of it"

How wrong I was!

CHAPTER SIX...THE EPILOGUE

I am not quite sure why 1974 was my last complete diary. I did start one in 1975 but stopped during the summer only to resume for the last two months of the year. The most probable reason was not taking my diary on holiday to Ibiza that year. Having broken the flow I got out of the habit of writing. I have however kept in touch with, and still see, a lot of the main players, which is really rewarding. Firstly, I will continue my story with Sue.

After an interesting Christmas Eve "date" we saw a lot of each other through 1975 whilst working together at The Leeds. We had a lot of fun but did not become an "item" until early 1976. Our relationship blossomed and prior to my first appointment as branch manager in Somerset we decided to get engaged, and then married in October 1979. We finally settled in Wetherby, West Yorkshire which we arrived at via Lichfield, North Ferriby and Holmes Chapel having had three children and one grandchild.

WHAT ELSE HAS CHANGED?

Central Grammar School for Boys

CGS became a comprehensive and amalgamated with Byng Kenrick Girl's Grammar School in 1974. In 2000 Sir Wilfrid Martineau was also included and the new school was named "The International School". It was refurbished in 2012 and now looks very modern. I discovered this when I visited with former pupils Keith Ingram and John Roden (who once lived opposite The Ringers) when we celebrated our 50th anniversary of starting at the school in September 2015.

The Ringers

In 1975 I worked behind the bar for several weeks whilst saving to buy a better car than the dodgy mini. It was much newer than the old mini but the street credibility of a Hillman Imp, even with metallic paint and the inevitable sports steering wheel, was fairly low. Tez also worked there and later met his first wife Gerry across the bar.

The Ringers survived until 2008 when it was finally closed down and scheduled to be replaced by housing. There was quite a delay during which time the building was vandalised and set on fire. However, it 'rose from the ashes' and I am pleased to report that the housing is now almost complete and as of April 2016 the detached houses are doing the site proud selling at c£285,000.

The Yew Tree, including the Rio

I was never keen on the Yew Tree pub, but the Rio was different, as it had housed the Sabbath Rock disco. The whole building was demolished in 2000 to be replaced by a shopping development including a new pub called the "Clumsy Swan". I have ventured in once and was pleased that my feet were no longer "glued" to the carpet. It was fairly spartan, had few clientele and large TV screens, a far cry from the lively hub of our youth and not really one for me. The Sabbath Rock disco temporally relocated to the Sportsman's Arms on the A45 near Coventry. The building is still there but since 2000 it has developed a new identity as The Quality Hotel.

Mothers, Music Venue, Erdington

When the lease above the furniture shop ran out Elton John was the last but one act to play at Mothers on 2nd January 1971. Quintessence closed the venue the following day. There was an attempt to reinvent it as "Stepmothers" based at the Belfry Hotel near Sutton Coldfield but perhaps unsurprisingly, it soon folded despite the appearance of Led Zeppelin in March 1971.

Sloopy's Nightclub

The club, situated in a basement on Corporation Street closed in 1982 when the licence expired after complaints of drunkenness being allowed on the premises. Such behaviour never happened when we were there!

Wragge & Co Solicitors

The affectionately known 'Wragges' is now a truly international law firm boasting 126 partners and over 500 lawyers. It went from strength to strength under the leadership of two of the lawyers who were there at the same time as me, namely: Pat Lawrence (later Sir Patrick) whose working group I was part of; and John Crabtree with whom I briefly shared an office. The firm has moved offices twice, first to Colmore Row and more recently to Snow Hill. In 2014 they merged with the London firm Lawrence Graham to create Wragge Lawrence Graham & Co.

The Leeds Permanent Building Society

The branch in Acocks Green doubled in size by swallowing the green grocers next door. The merger with the Halifax in 1995 led to massive changes for staff and customers. Today the office is still under the Halifax brand but following the collapse of HBOS is now part of the Lloyds Banking Group.

Political correctness (PC)

Life was definitely less PC in the early 70's. The TV programme Love Thy Neighbour starring Jack Smethurst and Rudolph Walker (now in Eastenders) would be slated for its racist attitudes and language. Although now we are much more relaxed about violence, sex and bad language on our screens.

Technology

There have been massive changes in this area. Back in 1970 only 35% of homes had a landline ("Stato" strikes again). At the start of 1970 there were only about 200,000 colour television sets in the UK. By 1972 this had risen to 1.6 million but they were limited to only three channels. The computer chip had just been invented but we had to wait a while for its impact on our daily lives. Back then there was no Internet, no home computers and no mobile phones.

Because we lived in a technological wilderness we had to plan things in advance, and we had to talk to each other. Was this better or worse? No emails to answer, no texts to misinterpret, no shopping online. Life was slower but in some ways easier.

Fashion

Fashion was pants! Loon pants and hot pants. I had a pair of crushed velvet loon pants, which were very "fetching". For the girls there were maxi skirts and mini skirts, and that's about the long and the short of it. When it came to cool hair it was long for the boys and perms for the girls.

Health

Smoking has fortunately gone out of fashion dropping from 45% of adults in 1974 to 16% in 2016, although the new trend of vaping has been introduced. Membership of gyms has grown massively as fitness becomes more important and less elite.

Medical advances have seen transplants become routine and the treatment of main killers such as cancer and heart disease become far more effective. My dad's fatal mitral valve problem would now be a simple routine replacement.

WHAT HASN'T CHANGED?

My friends

Even after more than forty years since my last diary entry, and living far away in Yorkshire I still keep in touch with the majority of the key characters who appeared in the five years from 1970.

Of the core gang only Gary (Gaz) has remained in Birmingham. John L is in Berkhamstead and Terry (Tez) has lived on the Isle of Wight for many years. The four of us try to meet up at least once a year and John and I have had some great trips in recent years to Turkey, Poland, Italy and Malta. Brian (Bri) lives in Chester and we have met up a couple of times. The only missing member is Paul W (Shrimp) who we think is back in Brum but must still be "putting his pumps on"!

I also meet up a couple of times a year with the Sheldon Heath boys - Martin (Tin), Steve C and Rob (Shez)- usually at Martin's in Wolverhampton where he and his wife Christine make us very welcome. Steve C travels up from Winchester and Rob from Bedford.

To keep up with the Central boys I travel back to Yardley a couple of times a year to meet up with John Roden, Keith Ingram, Graham (Gray) Buckley and Kim Rawson for a "Woolies night". This is held at Wetherspoons at the Yew Tree site in Yardley, which in our day was Woolworths. I also occasionally catch up with John Clegg at England cricket matches. He has lived in Chester for over forty years and has retired as a family division judge. He remains a loyal Blues fan as well as supporting Warwickshire cricket.

Terrorism

Unfortunately this still remains although the perpetrators have changed their causes. The world was a dangerous place in the 1970s and remains so today.

Wars still cause chaos and misery for many as they did in Vietnam. Blood is still spilt in the name of power or religion, just in different lands. It seems that nothing has been learnt.

Politics

Narrow elections, party strife and EU referendums are still the order of the day. No change there then! We now have the Greens, SNP and UKIP but the basics are the same.

The economy was in a poor state back then with the country effectively bankrupt and forced to seek a bail out from the IMF. Today the country still has record levels of debt and strikes are still experienced despite changes to labour laws.

On a lighter note

Aston Villa are back out of the top league (2016) but I still support them, albeit from my armchair. Unbelievably the Rolling Stones are STILL touring with virtually the same line up with some of them still fathering children!

WHAT HAVE I LEARNT?

Family

I was very fortunate to be born into a loving and caring family. Although the early loss of my dad was devastating, in some ways it made me stronger and encouraged me to make the most of life. My aunt and uncle lived the rest of their lives in the Isle of Man, both living into their late 80s. My grandad also had a good innings (86) and remained as cheerful as ever. Mum lived happily passed 90 before her dementia took hold. She never complained about anything and was pretty close to a perfect mum.

My brother Steve found happiness marrying Ann on his 40th birthday. Tragically Steve died of a sudden heart attack just four years later. Like my dad it was his one and only attack. I had spoken to him the night before when he complained of pains to his back and shoulders. It was however a different cause than the one claiming my dad. Ann and Steve were partners in a financial services training business which Ann continued to grow before eventually selling to Moodys. I am very grateful, as I know Steve would have been, for the fantastic support Ann gave to my mum taking her on holiday and making sure she was always safe and secure before mum moved to live in sheltered accommodation near to us.

Key decisions

Some decisions I made were life changing. Not staying on for 'A' levels turned out to be one of them. Leaving with six 'O' levels and starting at Wragge & Co worked out better for me than going to university as I discovered on a recent school reunion.

Turning down a very attractive offer to work for the Wellcome Foundation in favour of the Leeds Permanent Building Society was another good decision. The Leeds gave me an opportunity to enjoy a successful career both with them and later with the Halifax, and of course for meeting my wife. Sue has been a fantastic support touring the country via six houses at the same time raising three lovely children and now grandchildren.

I found following my instincts very helpful when making key decisions. If it feels right do it. If it doesn't, then don't, even if there are strong factors in favour like the car and money, as with the Wellcome offer.

I have also learnt the importance of making things happen. When I was managing my first branch in Bridgewater, Somerset I had heard that the Leeds was opening a branch in Cannock. Before taking up the manager's role at the

Bridgewater branch I had been Area Representative at Wolverhampton, charged with looking after our agents in Cannock, Boot and Son, which was one of the most successful in the country. It was clear to me that the new branch would be a business success from day one, and it was.

At the time the Leeds did not have an open selection process for promotion and no interviews were held. I decide to be a bit cheeky and write to my boss Mike Rooke asking for his support with Head Office. I dictated a letter pointing out why I should be considered for the post of Cannock manager, which Sue typed after the office had closed. She said that if she managed to type it without a single mistake I would get the job. She did and the job was mine! It was a roaring success and a great career stepping stone.

Would I change anything?

The simple answer is no. The five years between 1970 and 1975 were great fun and a tremendous development period, a broad and firm foundation for a successful career and life. Oh yes, there is one thing, perhaps three holidays in Skeggy was at least one too many, but all in all **NOT TOO BAD!**

Printed in Great Britain
by Amazon